The Intermediate Manual

A Handbook of Methods for Intermediate and Young People's Society Workers

by

R. P. Anderson

Managing Editor of the
Christian Endeavor World

First Fruits Press
Wilmore, Kentucky
c2015

The intermediate manual: a handbook of methods for intermediate and young people's society workers, by R. P. Anderson.

First Fruits Press, ©2015
Previously published: Boston, Chicago : United Society of Christian Endeavor ©1913.

ISBN: 9781621714132 (print), 9781621714149 (digital)

Digital version at http://place.asburyseminary.edu/christianendeavorbooks/5/

First Fruits Press is a digital imprint of the Asbury Theological Seminary, B.L. Fisher Library. Asbury Theological Seminary is the legal owner of the material previously published by the Pentecostal Publishing Co. and reserves the right to release new editions of this material as well as new material produced by Asbury Theological Seminary. Its publications are available for noncommercial and educational uses, such as research, teaching and private study. First Fruits Press has licensed the digital version of this work under the Creative Commons Attribution Noncommercial 3.0 United States License. To view a copy of this license, visit http://creativecommons.org/licenses/by-nc/3.0/us/.

For all other uses, contact:

First Fruits Press
B.L. Fisher Library
Asbury Theological Seminary
204 N. Lexington Ave.
Wilmore, KY 40390
http://place.asburyseminary.edu/firstfruits

Anderson, Robert Phillips, 1866-
    The intermediate manual : a handbook of methods for intermediate and young people's society workers / by R.P. Anderson..
    180 pages ; 21 cm.
    Wilmore, Ky. : First Fruits Press, ©2015.
    Reprint. Previously published: Boston : United Society of Christian Endeavor, ©1913.
    ISBN: 9781621714132 (pbk.)
1. United Society of Christian Endeavor. I. Title.
BV1426 .A6 2015

Cover design by Jonathan Ramsay

asburyseminary.edu
800.2ASBURY
204 North Lexington Avenue
Wilmore, Kentucky 40390

First Fruits Press
The Academic Open Press of Asbury Theological Seminary
204 N. Lexington Ave., Wilmore, KY 40390
859-858-2236
first.fruits@asburyseminary.edu
asbury.to/firstfruits

The Intermediate Manual

A Handbook of Methods for Intermediate and Young People's Society Workers

BY

R. P. ANDERSON

*Managing Editor of
The Christian Endeavor World*

International Society of Christian Endeavor
Boston and Chicago

Copyrighted, 1913, by the
United Society of Christian Endeavor

1MX1X29
PRINTED IN U. S. A.

Foreword

RELIGIOUS workers desire to make men and women out of the material that they find in the community. The task is a difficult one at best, but its difficulties are immensely increased if workers plunge into their labors badly equipped and with only a vague idea of the means they are going to employ to attain their end.

There is no excuse for Sunday-school workers' remaining in ignorance of the work in which they are engaged. There are books a plenty dealing with the problem from every conceivable angle. But it is different with the Intermediate Christian Endeavor society. Here and there articles have appeared about it. Talks have been made about it at conventions. But no handbook which might serve superintendents as a guide has thus far been published.

The Intermediate society is an instrument for the making of manhood and womanhood. The aim of the following pages is to give superintendents a working idea of methods to employ and of the nature of the young people with whom they will have to labor. The success of the society will always depend more or less on the superintendent and the way in which he leads. There can be little success without some knowledge of adolescent human nature and of plans to follow.

Intermediates can do most of the things that are done in the Young People's society. The difference between the two societies lies in the peculiar mental state of adolescent boys and girls. This must be studied and mastered. The superintendent will be guide, counsellor, and friend, a true leader and not a driver. And his success may be measured by the strength of the confidence with which he can inspire the young people. After all, the deepest secret of leadership is love.

R. P. ANDERSON.

Contents

I.	THE PLACE OF THE INTERMEDIATE SOCIETY IN THE CHURCH	7
II.	THE QUESTION OF LEADERSHIP	18
III.	SOME THINGS THE SUPERINTENDENT OUGHT TO KNOW: *A. The Mental State*	27
IV.	SOME THINGS THE SUPERINTENDENT OUGHT TO KNOW: *B. The Religious State*	34
V.	GOLDEN RULES FOR SUPERINTENDENTS	42
VI.	ORGANIZATION	50
VII.	HOW TO MAKE SUCCESSFUL MEETINGS	72
VIII.	BIBLE DRILLS	85
IX.	COMMITTEES AT WORK: *The Prayer-Meeting Committee*	99
X.	COMMITTEES AT WORK: *The Lookout Committee*	109
XI.	COMMITTEES AT WORK: *The Missionary Committee*	120
XII.	COMMITTEES AT WORK: *The Social Committee*	131

CONTENTS

XIII. COMMITTEES AT WORK: *Flower, Pastor's Aid, Information, Sunday-school, Junior, Good Literature, Temperance and Good Citizenship, Music, Whatsoever, Delegation, Publicity* . . 145

XIV. THINGS THAT MAY BE DONE . . 152

XV. INCREASING EFFICIENCY . . . 169

The Intermediate Manual

CHAPTER I

THE PLACE OF THE INTERMEDIATE SOCIETY IN THE CHURCH

THERE is a period in the lives of most boys and girls when they do not seem to belong anywhere.

Very likely they rebel at the Sunday-school. If they have attended the Junior Christian Endeavor society, they have outgrown it. Many of its methods that once satisfied them, and that still satisfy younger children, appear to them too juvenile. They feel the strange impulse of a larger, richer life.

No longer at home in the Junior society, they are also strangers in the Young People's society. In the presence of older people they feel awkward and timid, burdened with a sense of inferiority, however much they try to hide it. If they have been active as Junior Endeavorers and have graduated into the Young People's society, they are nevertheless liable to fall into ways of silence. The delightful freedom that characterized them as children has gone from them, and they are oppressed with self-consciousness and fear.

So they frequently drop out of Christian Endeavor altogether.

One of the startling things that should give the church pause is the fact that more boys are lost to organized Christianity between the ages of fourteen and twenty than at any other age. It is easy, it seems, to drift from the moorings of childhood, and hard to find another anchorage.

At a ministers' meeting in Philadelphia one of the pastors present made the remark that the people of the slums are the lost sheep of our own household. Another pastor challenged the statement, and several ministers were appointed to inquire into the situation.

Among them was Rev. J. Wilbur Chapman, D. D., then pastor of Bethany Presbyterian Church. Speaking of his experiences in investigating the early religious affiliations of dwellers in the city's slums, he said: "One of the worst women I have ever seen I met at three o'clock in the morning in one of Philadelphia's slums. When I told her that I came from Bethany, she said: 'Bethany! My mother carried me there in her arms. I went for years to Bethany Sunday-school. I sat in Miss Brown's class, half a dozen rows from the front.'

"She paused as the tears stole down her

THE INTERMEDIATE SOCIETY

cheeks. Dreams of sweet and innocent childhood flashed across her sin-scarred mind. Then she brushed the tears away.

"'You let me slip,' she trembled. 'You let me slip!'"

And that is the history of untold thousands. The church has somehow, in spite of herself, let them slip.

This outward drift beyond boundaries set in childhood is not, however, confined to the church. It is present in school life, although conditions have partly blinded us to the fact. Dr. G. Stanley Hall, writing about the period of adolescence, or the transition from boyhood into manhood, remarks:

"This is the age when they (*i. e.*, boys) drop out of school in far too large numbers, and Stableton thinks that the small percentage of male graduates from our high schools is due to the inability of the average grammar-grade or high-school teacher to deal rightly with boys in this critical period of their school life."

"The weakest work in our schools," writes Stableton, "is the handling of boys entering the adolescent period of life, and there is no greater blessing that can come to a boy at this age, when he does not understand himself, than a good strong teacher that understands him, has faith in him, and will day by day lead him until he can walk alone."

The luxurious growth of so many organizations designed for boys and girls of this transition period is proof that the church is now aware of the need of some means of stopping its loss from the ranks of its young people.

Rev. A. Z. Conrad, D. D., of Boston, when pastor in Worcester, Mass., saw that Juniors, automatically pushed into the Young People's society when they became too old for the Junior society, found that social relations were fixed and that the activities of the society were already well manned. Dr. Conrad found, further, that there were many boys and girls in church and Sunday-school who had passed the Junior age, yet could not be prevailed upon to join the older society. To meet the need of this class on the one hand, and of graduating Juniors on the other, Dr. Conrad organized an Intermediate society among his young people, and his example has been followed by many pastors in all parts of this country and also in foreign lands.

The Intermediate society is indeed the logical link between Junior and Young People's societies. If the training of children begins in a Junior society, it is reasonable on the face of it that that training should continue without a break, just as we organize our secular schools so that one builds upon the foundation laid by another.

THE INTERMEDIATE SOCIETY   11

No one has the least doubt but some sort of organization is needed for young people in the transition period. The only question is the kind of organization that will accomplish most.

It seems to us self-evident that to take a Junior out of the Junior society and usher him into an entirely different kind of organization, whether it be a boys' club, Boy Scouts, Knights of King Arthur, or any other association, manifestly breaks the sequence of his training. It switches him to a new track. He loses impetus. The environment is new, and he must adjust himself to it. He has lost the things among which he has long moved.

But take a boy from a Junior society, and place him in an Intermediate society, and he advances along lines with which he is familiar. There is no break. He has direct use for the very things that he has learned among the Juniors. And the same is true of girls.

If it is objected that by introducing a boy into another kind of organization we thereby enrich his life and experience, the obvious reply is the question, At what cost?

There is nothing in any other organization that cannot be used along with Christian Endeavor. The society has proved itself adaptable enough, and the chief features of practically every boys' and girls' organization that claims recognition may very easily be carried out as a part of Intermediate Christian Endeavor work.

The break in training, the loss of the distinctive Christian Endeavor pledge, and not infrequently the loss of the distinctively religious element, make the abandonment of Christian Endeavor for young people in the adolescent stage altogether too dangerous an experiment.

For we must not forget that Christian Endeavor frankly makes the religious appeal. The Intermediate age—fourteen to eighteen or twenty—is recognized by all psychologists as the age of decision. Destinies are then made. Young people that are led to take a definite stand for Christ during this period usually grow into Christian men and women. The boys and girls that wander at this age often wander long and far.

What are we doing to hold them in this dangerous time?

While we recognize the worth, as accessories, of many schemes advanced, like the Boys' Brigade, Boy Scouts, and so forth, we believe that the supreme and vital influence in any young life is the influence of religion. And Christian Endeavor stands for religion. This is central.

Christian Endeavor stands for a pledged life, a devotional life, and a useful life.

Through the tumultuous years of adolescence, when boys and girls are finding themselves when everything about them is in solution, but ready to crystallize, religion is the most potent influence to help them to form their ideals aright and " come to themselves." Let them feel that they are pledged and that Christ owns them, let them feel in those eager years that they are here to be useful, and lead them into the habit of daily prayer and Bible-reading, and you have helped them to a position where they can stand safely sheltered until the storm sweeps past.

If a church once loosens its grip on its young people, if it lets them drift into some outside organization, good enough in its way, but one that does not keep the boy and girl keyed up to definite Christian work, the probability is that it will lose them later so far as church-work is concerned. Let the Junior Endeavorer become homeless, and his enthusiasm will soon cool. He will get out of practice. If he works for the new club or order which for any reason he has joined, he will grow to love it, if he sticks to it. And that is well. But in a year or two try to get him to attend the Christian Endeavor society, or to do definite work for the Master; and in too many cases you will find that the boy has lost his interest in the religious aspect of life.

This is the point where many beautiful theories of the adolescent age fail in practice. Tender solicitation not to spoil the fair flower of natural development by the rough hand of direction frequently leads the boy or girl to lose taste for religious work altogether.

It is not self-evident that the club or the lodge is the stepping-stone to the church.

The club or lodge may be used to help, but it never can be the central influence in the formation of *Christian* character.

The world is not going to be saved, nor the church built up, nor the heathen evangelized, by clubs, but by workers that are aflame with Pentecostal fire.

If the period of adolescence is the impressionable age, when it is easier than at any other time to form religious ideals, why should we not seek to gather our young people into an organization that provides these ideals so simply, directly, and steadily as the Intermediate Christian Endeavor society?

The worth of the Young People's society is proved by its fruits. The Junior society has found a place in the church, and is accomplishing good work. That is to say, experience shows that Christian Endeavor fits both children and adults.

Why should it not also fit young men or women in their teens?

Wherever Intermediate Christian Endeavor has been fairly tried and wisely superintended, good results have followed. Indeed, a large part of its usefulness depends upon the superintendent. With a consecrated worker in charge, a worker that knows something about young people, their difficulties, their aspirations, and their ideals, the society will lend itself to high purposes, and will surely lead young lives to Jesus Christ.

" I rode on the train last night with a boy," says Dr. Lapsley A. McAfee. " He plans that his manhood shall be one of strength and credit. No, that is not quite fair to him. He expects such an experience. He is not planning for it, but expects it to come to him.

" He is now nineteen years of age, according to the old family Bible at home. But he was so strong of vile whiskey last night that he could hardly follow my talk, and he has been cultivating that habit for five years. Unless he became a victim of some rascal in the city last night he is probably in the train to-day running toward his home in one of the Southern States.

" Now, he had an idea that he could finish up a quart bottle not yet opened, but laid away in his suitcase, within a day or two, and then be ready for inspection by the time he reaches home. I had to tell him how his face showed his dissipation, and I urged that he throw the bottle out of the car-window that his face might have all the chance possible to clear up.

"Of course, I told him as plainly as I could of the One who could clean his life, his will, and his whole self. His trouble is that he does not realize that he is in the Intermediate age, 'in the middle between' childhood and manhood. He does not see that his present stage has definite relationship to that which is to follow. Poor boy! He does not yet know how much easier it is to slide down hill than to climb up."

But the church knows, and its business is to give its young people something that will not only prevent them from sliding down, but that will help them to climb up. The boy was all wrong in his answer to the teacher's question, "What little boys go to heaven?" "Dead ones," he shouted.

He was wrong. It is the live ones. The dead ones that glide with the current go anywhere except to heaven.

Intermediate Christian Endeavor has a special place in a city church. The pull away from church influences is particularly strong in cities. The theatre and the moving-picture show must be counteracted by entertainments that Intermediates are usually only too anxious to get up themselves. The alluring dance must be fought with clean socials. The craving for outdoor activity must be met by clubs and games and weekly hikes. Some churches have pastors

THE INTERMEDIATE SOCIETY 17

whose sole duty is to attend to the young life of the church and community. The way they succeed is sufficient proof that boys and girls of Intermediate age are ready to respond to the church that understands them and works for them.

CHAPTER II

THE QUESTION OF LEADERSHIP

YOUNG men or young women in the early twenties may not have so large a fund of wisdom or so fine judgment as a man of forty or fifty ; but, if they are endowed with average common sense, and know that they do not know everything, and if they are truly consecrated to the Master's service, they will make acceptable and efficient Intermediate superintendents.

They are nearer boyhood or girlhood than an older person. They have not forgotten the young person's point of view. They do not wear the brow of care. The struggles, the trials, the disappointments, and the aspirations of youth are still fresh in their minds. They know boys and girls, and therefore can manage them better than one that has partly forgotten what it is to be young. On the other hand, let us not forget that many older people retain the freshness of youth, and are ideal superintendents.

The leaders of the Intermediate society should normally come from the Young People's society. The Intermediate age, so vital for the

THE QUESTION OF LEADERSHIP 19

individual and the church, should be a problem so close to the heart of all pastors that they would gladly undertake to help to train leaders for the boys and girls. The Young People's society can supply the material.

The ideal arrangement would be to have in every church a group of men and women that are interested in Intermediate work,—that is, in work with young people in their teens,— who will seek leaders for the Intermediates, see to their proper training, and stand behind them with counsel and in other ways. If this is impossible, then the Young People's society should step into the gap and fill it in the best way it can.

At present workers with young people are trained very much as boys used to be taught how to swim. The teacher threw them overboard, and told them to strike out. This method works in some cases yet, not because it has any real worth as a method, but because of the grit of the learner.

Superintendents ought to be taught some of the problems that they will be sure to encounter. They must know the main history of adolescence and its storm and stress, and they must have a saving knowledge of the fact that what counts most with young people is less what a superintendent says than what he is and does. Superintendents that hope to succeed must learn how to approach the boy or girl from every angle: from the physical side, through games and gymnastic exercises; from the intellectual side, through the young person's insatiable thirst for knowledge; from the social side, through social opportunities; and from the religious side, through the vital influence of personal example.

The wise superintendent will, of course, have a definite aim for his ministry. To flounder along in a haphazard way means sure disappointment and failure. One young man held himself to his ideals by writing the following aims in his note-book, frequently refreshing his memory by reading them over and examining himself on each one. He sought

1. To inspire his Intermediates to a definite purpose in life.

2. To kindle high ambitions so as to make the most of every life in his care.

3. To encourage the young people to overcome obstacles and to know that by overcoming them new strength was gained.

4. To inspire self-confidence and initiative.

In numberless ways he brought these lessons before the society. He would drive one point home by means of a story from a magazine, or by referring to a newspaper item. He found that truth could be impressed on the mind better by giving concrete instances than by merely stating abstract principles. He did not preach. None of the boys and girls knew that he was trying to implant seeds of truth in their minds. They only realized that he was interesting, that he was alive, and that there was something doing in the society. But they learned the lessons that he taught.

The first qualification for an Intermediate superintendent is that he or she be consecrated. The society tends to become like its leader. If the superintendent be worldly in thought and manner, the seeds of such worldliness will be sown in the hearts of the young people. This frequently happens before we realize what is taking place; and then we wonder why the spirit of consecration, devotion, and reverence has departed from the young people of the church.

It is vital to have a genuine practising Christian, and not merely a professing Christian, at the head of an Intermediate society. The life of the superintendent, whether man or woman, must be pure and above reproach. His thought must be spiritual; his habits must be clean; his example must be worthy of imitation.

His motto should be, "By love serve." He must know how the young people look at things, and he must sympathize with their point of view. When a man feels that his position as superintendent is a task, he is setting forth upon the road to failure. Service is opportunity. To be charged with the power of influencing future members of the church and future citizens of the nation is a privilege that might make angels envious. If a man has vision, he can find sustenance and joy in labor.

Many an earnest superintendent suffers shipwreck on the question of authority. To young children authority is the most natural thing in the world; but adolescents strain at the leash of parental control, and will more readily follow the lead of an outsider.

This fact gives the superintendent his clew. The authority he must strive to gain, however, is not that of bit and bridle and rein, but that of firm, sweet reasonableness. The appeal to reason which enlists the boy's will, which makes him the arbiter in his own case,—a principle employed successfully in juvenile republics,—is the only kind of authority that the Intermediate will endure. He respects the man that knows and that can. He accepts authority based upon demonstrated knowledge, and will follow it to the world's end.

A superintendent, on the other hand, may very easily stultify his best efforts by a show of suspicion, severity, solemnness, sarcasm, or by scolding. If he expects to curb the exuberance of youth by threats, he is doomed to ignominious defeat. If the young people get the idea that a promise on his lips is not sacred, his power over them is gone.

Intermediates are quick to detect injustice, and sometimes the superintendent's temptation is strong in this direction. Some young men, and, for that part, some young women, are exasperating, and more so if they see that the superintendent is exasperated. It is easy, and sometimes delightful, to bear down upon offenders a little more heavily than is right. A fatal error, and one that brings swift punishment in loss of respect! Malice can never be hid. The cruel sneer, the bitter gibe, the attempt to hold an offender up to ridicule, are sure to swing back with deadly force upon the superintendent that indulges in such dangerous pleasantries.

The Intermediate age is the age of chivalry, of heroism, of generosity; the period when a young man's sympathy is easily enlisted for the under dog. It does not matter that the under dog is a cur that has been misbehaving and that is getting exactly what it deserves. Boys jump to conclusions. The obvious fact is that the under dog is yowling, and they want to call the victor off.

Discipline can be maintained in many societies by organizing them on the principle of a juvenile republic, letting the members themselves, through an organized court of discipline, be both judge and jury.

Indeed, the superintendent should follow the advice of the old fisherman who gave a receipt for success in angling. He had three rules. The first was, "Keep out of sight." The second was, "Keep farther out of sight." And the third ran, "Keep still farther out of sight."

The question is sometimes asked whether a superintendent should be a man or a woman.

We must remember that the aim of an Intermediate superintendent is not merely to be a leader of a meeting or a director of work, but an adviser of souls. He is in closer touch with young people than the busy pastor can hope to be. He is more likely to be made a confidant than even the pastor.

But there are difficulties that come up in a young girl's experience that she cannot make known to a male superintendent; and there are troubles that strike a boy that he will not confide to a woman. It is possible, of course, that there are other organizations in the church that can supply guidance to both boys and girls, but in most churches a superintendent is likely to be closer to the young people than other workers.

It seems that we cannot well dispense with the virile strength that comes from the presence of a man in the society; nor, on the other hand, can we do without the sweetness and tact that woman brings to her tasks. The ideal society will probably have two superintendents, a man and a woman, each doing work that will naturally fall among those of his or her own sex. The two leaders will plan together and share the responsibility. They are there to superintend, not to execute. They will both keep themselves in the background, giving the Intermediates right of way.

Where there are a number of young people of Intermediate age, and it is impossible to find a male superintendent, a capable woman should take the lead.

The superintendent's path is not strewn with roses. He will collide with difficulties, and there will be occasions when he will need all his tact to get around obstacles or over slippery places. But it is worth while. It means the saving of souls and the saving of young lives.

Some time ago, when a statue of George Peabody, the philanthropist, was unveiled in London, the sculptor, Mr. Story, was called upon to make a speech. He touched the statue with his hand twice, and twice he repeated the words: "This is my speech! This is my speech!"

The superintendent's supreme happiness is, in after-years, to look upon his boys or his girls and say with Paul, "Ye are my joy and my crown of rejoicing."

We have been speaking as if the superintendent were nearly always a man. As a matter of fact more superintendents are women. The same rules apply, however, to both sexes in their work with young people.

CHAPTER III

SOME THINGS THE SUPERINTENDENT OUGHT TO KNOW

A. *The Mental State*

IN the years of adolescence boys and girls differ somewhat in their mental and spiritual development, but both sexes are in the melting-pot. In a short time something will emerge from that crucible that will solidify into habit of thought and action. The superintendent, if he or she is to attain to efficiency, must know what is taking place in the minds of young persons, and must provide a mould in which to shape the character.

The physical changes that occur in this period often provide a clew to a correct diagnosis of mental disturbances, and will suggest the remedy. A reliable book on adolescence should be procured and studied. "The Psychology of Religion," by E. D. Starbuck, is an excellent guide. It is sold by the United Society of Christian Endeavor, Tremont Temple, Boston, Mass., at $1.50, postage 12 cents extra.

One of the marked results of the physical change referred to is seen in a new relation of the sexes. Broadly speaking, a young child is sexless in its relations with others. As the stirrings of sex begin to make themselves felt, the youth suddenly realizes that he is attracted in a new, strange manner to the opposite sex, and the age of romance opens wide its doors.

We speak of the boy, but the same things are true of girls.

They dream dreams in solitude. Wonderful aspirations move within the soul. The world is bathed in glory reflected from their hopes, and at the same time they know the happy pangs of unsatisfied longing.

As for the boy, sometimes a thirst for fame consumes him. He is deeply stirred by glorious deeds of old-time chivalry or of modern achievement. He longs for action, adventure, romance. Perhaps he desires leadership, the joy of initiating action. He feels that the time for play is past, and he wants to undertake worthy enterprises that will tax and test his strength. He pictures to himself the delight of receiving the plaudits of friends for work well done. He wants the good will of all the world.

In both boys and girls the sense of self arises. As children they moved around totally unconscious of themselves, with the sweet simplicity and naturalness of wild creatures of the woods. But, as self-consciousness develops, naturalness

THE MENTAL STATE 29

is inhibited. They become awkward. They cannot walk across a room if others are watching them. Their feet are in the way, and refuse the commands of the brain. All actions are forced, because consciously directed; and are liable to become artificial.

Youth becomes aware, too, of a world around it. Girls begin earlier than boys to attend to matters of dress. Pride awakens. In the boy it is less the love of pretty things that moves him than the feeling that people are watching him and criticising him. Unless he is careful he may contract bad habits while in this mental state, habits that will last a lifetime. He may, for example, dress loudly, drift into dandyism, put on airs, develop conceit, become affected in deportment. He may have a bad attack, attended by all these symptoms, and more, all at once; or he may develop the symptoms one by one, and in varying combinations.

A good many morbid conditions may attend the period of adolescence. Boys are liable to have severe attacks of doubt,—although girls are by no means exempt,—while girls are liable to brood and be tortured with oversensitiveness. Fear, too, is one of the most common accompaniments of youth. It manifests itself in all degrees, from timidity and modesty to that appalling sense of inferiority that makes a boy shun all company. Fear in some form is at the bottom of the habit of blushing in the presence of strangers. The very worst thing one can do is to ridicule the victim of this obsession. The habit may be overcome by helping the boy or girl to realize that there is no real reason for blushing or for sensitiveness, that the trouble lies in having too vivid an imagination, and that fear-thought can be put aside and conquered.

When fear or timidity drives young people into solitude and silence, they must be drawn back by gentleness and tact. "The tendency to solitude at adolescence indicates no fulness, but want." It is not a mark of greatness. It is the sign of a troubled soul.

It is well to remember that every impression made on the mind in these years is deep and lasting. This is especially true of impressions that wound. Derision is felt with a keenness that is mercifully dulled in older people. They "don't care." But the youth cares intensely. Censure cuts like a whip. Failure to make good in any direction depresses with crushing force. A dog that gets licked once has not much taste for another scrap. When a boy or girl goes down to failure, we need not rub salt into the wound.

The superintendent should understand not only the morbid states of adolescence, but also the budding powers of youth; and he should seek to direct them. A great deal of youthful crime is simply misdirected energy. Jane Addams shows that one of the strongest instincts of the boy is to perform daring feats, and that these feats often bring him into violent collision with the law. The energy that prompts such feats may be turned into safe channels. The gymnasium, the baseball-field, and the hike provide fine outlets. The desire for combat, the wish to pit his powers against others, may be satisfied in debate. The lust for glory and distinction may be appeased by giving the youth a chance to see what he can accomplish in elocution and oratory. The natural love of the spectacular may be gratified by letting Intermediates get up plays, pageants, and socials; and the innate passion for chivalry and honor may be fed by adopting some of the best features of such organizations as the Boy Scouts.

At no age are pity and sympathy so easily aroused as during this period. The normal youth hates oppression, and desires fair play with all his soul. Here is a foundation for virtues that make good citizens. Love of fair play can be developed into honesty and honor, and pity and sympathy can be transformed into charity, benevolence, kindness, and good will.

Again, the years of adolescence mark the period when a larger life dawns upon the mind, when young people learn that they must live along with others as part of a great world. They choose their companions. They feel that they are not sufficient unto themselves, and they crave the stimulating influence of friends, if they are normal in their growth.

Adolescence means for youth a complete change of mental base. A child's thought is entirely different from the thought of a young person in his teens. "When I was a child, I thought as a child . . . but, when I became a man, I put away childish things." The Intermediate years mark the transition.

It is sad to see well-meaning parents handle their sons and daughters that have reached the age of adolescence as if they were children. How often we hear the wail, "Johnny has become unmanageable," when the fact is that the parents have forgotten that Johnny is no longer a child. He is budding into manhood; and, like a growing plant, he should be helped to grow according to his nature, and not according to the nature of either father or mother.

Instead of tightening the reins they should be loosened. The child is guided by command, but the young man and the young woman will not take orders in the conduct of life. They wish to be guided from within, from reason and conscience. When Frances Willard reached her eighteenth birthday, she resolved that she should conduct her life, not according to the desire of her parents, but according to her own conscience. Her father had prohibited her from reading novels; so on this day she took Scott's "Ivanhoe" to the porch, and sat down to read it. Very soon her father came along. "What is that you are reading?" "Ivanhoe." "But have I not forbidden you to read novels?" "Yes, but, father, you are forgetting what day this is." "What has the day got to do with the deed?" "I am eighteen to-day, and of age. From to-day on, I need not obey any laws but the law of God and my conscience. I believe that 'Ivanhoe' is a good book to read, and I am reading it." For a moment the astonished father did not know what to do. Then common sense prevailed. He called his daughter's statement a declaration of independence, and said that together they would try to keep the laws of God.

The superintendent can be companion, counsellor, and friend, and can do much to educate reason and conscience. One may suggest, guide, talk over problems, relate experiences; but dictate, never.

CHAPTER IV

SOME THINGS THE SUPERINTENDENT OUGHT TO KNOW

B. *The Religious State*

THE attitude of a young person in his teens toward religion is very different from that of a child.

The most marked characteristic of a child's religion is credulity. The Junior believes what is told him, literally and without hesitation. His faith is absolute, unless he has "found out" his elders or caught them in prevarication; and even then the tendency is for him to trust the word of older people in matters of religion.

But it is different with the adolescent. The simple, unreasoning faith of childhood gives place to a desire to examine, reason, understand. Faith tends to become personal. The young man wants to see with his own eyes. The ego outgrows traditional beliefs, and claims its right to get into first-hand contact with reality.

The shifting of base from authority to personal responsibility is the cause of many of the peculiar phenomena of adolescence. The Junior believes, imitates, obeys—although there are exceptions to this general rule. He lives near to God and the spiritual world. To him God is real, no matter how conceived; and consequently prayer is easy and natural. Of course, if a child's training has been wrong, the little one may grow up with a great fear of God; but it can be just as easily trained to love Him.

The longer a child can remain in this state of simple, balanced faith, the better will it be for it. For childhood is the period of assimilation. Example has a profound and lasting influence. The Junior drinks in the best things that come to him, and they enter into his character.

This, too, is the period of love. Love is the dominating feeling of the child mind. If that basic love be appealed to by more love and kindness, there will be a generous response. This is the reason why kindness is a more potent factor in the education of a boy than is punishment; kindness makes a bid for love; punishment is an appeal to fear. If a Junior fails to manifest due reverence and awe,—a matter about which many good people are exercised,—it is well to remember that the reason probably is that the Junior's mind is void of fear. It is best not to attempt to awaken awe in such a mind. The love appeal, which is absolutely fearless, is by far the more powerful. You can get more out of a man that loves God than you can get out of one whose motive is fear.

Starbuck points out, what we must all have noticed, "that religion is distinctively external to a child rather than something that possesses inner significance." One of his correspondents remarks: "I was counselled to love and fear God, and to obey every word in the Holy Scriptures. This God was part of my childhood, always present, though never near. He never entered into my life, but remained outside, and kept His eye upon it."

Adolescence brings with it a great awakening and often a realization of God. The hazy ideas of childhood clarify. Sometimes the awakening is accompanied by an emotional crisis, an explosion that starts the soul in a new direction. This is conversion.

Try to conceive adolescence as a growth into manhood or womanhood. When we read about the storm and stress of this period, we must beware lest we think that such disturbances are absolutely indispensable. They are no more necessary than are growing-pains for a growing boy. All growth should be painless, and would be if we did not violate some law or other. The young life should pass from childhood to manhood or to womanhood without friction and distress. Therefore it is well to seek to make the process as smooth and painless as possible. Trouble often comes, however, from the soul's finding difficulty in adapting

THE RELIGIOUS STATE 37

itself to its new environment. We perform a great service if we can keep the young person steady during the process of adaptation.

We have said that there is a close relation between the physical and the mental states. It follows that the more normal and healthy the body is, the easier will be mental, moral, and spiritual adjustments. Hence we should give attention to exercise, outdoor games, fresh air, good circulation of the blood, free respiration, and whatever makes large calls upon physical energy.

There are two outstanding facts in the life of a young man which every Intermediate superintendent should bear in mind: first, he exhibits an increased activity; and second, he suffers from a reaction.

With the growth of the body a fund of nervous energy seems to be released, resulting in both physical and mental activity. In some cases this leads to adventures with the gang. Wherever it is present, and it is sure to be present in an Intermediate society, the superintendent should seek wisely to direct it by suggesting channels through which it may flow. Very often the Intermediates will furnish him with clews for suggestions, for it is always best to work along with the normal desires of young people.

Periods of enlargement and activity are sure

to be followed by corresponding periods of indifference. The superintendent that has no knowledge of what is taking place easily becomes discouraged, and thinks that his work is in vain if his workers appear to lose interest. He presses the young man, it may be, to renewed activity; possibly he accuses him of callousness; and, if he is not careful, he may end in driving him away.

The wise course is to give line. The cause of the indifference is simply exhaustion, a condition of which the subject himself is serenely unaware and at which, if it were suggested to him, he would laugh scornfully. If he is wisely let alone,—of course he must not be lost sight of,—the life-forces will return and demand expression. Therefore, when an Intermediate grows cold, simply keep in touch to see that he does not drift into evil; but do not press him to work. He will want work when he is ready.

This nervous exhaustion, which claims a period of rest, explains the brooding depression, the morbid introspection, and the burdening sense of inferiority that torture the adolescent. It also supplies the key to those fits of anger and irritation, hatefulness, self-will, and defiance that appear so serious in the eyes of onlookers.

Sympathetic understanding of this state of soul will suggest to superintendents both what to do and what not to do. For instance, when a soul is in the depths already, crushed and oppressed, it is fatal to seek to impress upon it a sense of unworthiness and sin, and of the horrors of punishment. It may even do harm to place too much emphasis upon ideals. What is needed is that we stimulate the weak and distrustful, tide over the period of rest, and help to arouse the mind, in due time, to renewed effort.

Psychologists speak of a period of alienation when the young person is oppressed by a feeling of discord with his environment, and holds himself aloof. The root reason for this may be the reaction of which we have been speaking, or alienation may be caused by the soul's honest effort to think out and solve its own problems. The young man and woman are growing more and more independent. Freedom is their life. They are analyzing, reasoning, rejecting convention and tradition, trying to get a standpoint of their own, eager to attain the truth.

In the earlier stages of adolescence the mind is somewhat like a ship driven hither and thither by conflicting winds; but in the later period the captain is on board trying to steer aright.

The boy or girl that finds the world of childhood shattered by contact with modern science should not be looked upon with horror as a monster, but with deepest sympathy. It is not necessary, of course, that doubts come. A new world may be organized without an earthquake throwing the old one into chaos. But, if doubts arrive, it is necessary that we understand why they come and how to treat them. It is common enough nowadays to find young people that doubt the inspiration of the Bible, the divinity of Christ, the miracles of the Old and New Testaments, the story of the creation, and so forth; and here and there one may even find one that questions the very existence of God.

If we meet the doubter with expressions of dismay, we establish him in his unbelief. Doubt should be welcomed as a sign of health. Its function is to make us continually revise our knowledge and thus discover new truths. If we show that we are glad that a young man has begun to doubt, because this evidences thought, we disarm him at the start. Then we can talk matters over with him, draw him out, and suggest points of view of which, perhaps, he has never dreamed.

Since adolescence is a period of activity a young person's religion must be made a religion of doing, and doing things that are worth while. Intermediates should not be burdened with a decalogue of "don'ts." The pledge, "I will strive to do," expresses their natural feelings.

No two boys or girls are alike. Storm and stress in the experience of different individuals will vary very materially. We need not look for all the phenomena of adolescence in one life. No young man could carry such a burden. We must study each case by itself; we must win the confidence of the Intermediates; and we shall find, before we know it, that we are helping beyond our fondest hopes. The superintendent who is comrade and friend will surely win both respect and lasting love.

CHAPTER V

GOLDEN RULES FOR SUPERINTENDENTS

It may not be amiss to gather together a few rules based on experience that may help workers to thread the labyrinth of Intermediate work.

1. Be constructive. In this period of adjustment boys and girls are building a new world. Do not demolish their house, even if it be a house of cards, by criticism of any kind. When it falls, assist them to erect another and a better.

2. Study the physical nature of the boys and girls. The physical state is intimately connected with the mental state. Clean bodily habits are necessary if we are to have clean souls. Lay the foundation of sound living by imparting instruction regarding the evils of alcohol and tobacco, the necessity of plenty of sound sleep, hygiene, and so on. Young people want to know about their bodies. Tell them.

3. Study the young people's way of thinking. How many of us can tell how our friends make decisions, whether they move by impulse or by reason, and, if by reason, what kind of reason? Here is a boy or a girl that drifts when he or she is forced to choose. He or she obeys the pull of the tide. Here is one that follows his companions. One is reckless; another is determined; yet another weighs the matter from the moral point of view. There is a habit of decision, formed in youth. Watch the young person's habit forming, and guide it. That is the way to make character.

4. *Train the will to do right.* There are people whose decisions are flabby, and topple over when they are touched by argument. Teach the boy or girl to will to do right, and then, having made the decision, to stick to it though the heavens fall. Illustrations a plenty will be found in business life. Many a young man is ruined because he acquiesces in evil in his business relations. He sees evil done so often that he grows accustomed to it; his conscience becomes drugged; and before he knows it he is guilty of the same practices that he formerly condemned.

5. *Study young folks' fads.* A superintendent that brought a small collection of butterflies to the meeting one evening for an object-talk was astonished to see the most unruly boy in the society absorbed in the pretty insects. The superintendent promptly invited the boy to his home, and a real friendship was struck, which lasted through delightful years. Enter intelligently into a boy's or a girl's fads. If you do

not understand what they are interested in, they will teach you with pleasure.

6. *Co-operate with the parents.* The home often shirks its duty. Visit the parents when the boy or girl is not present, and secure their co-operation in helping the young people. The home is too important an ally to be neglected.

7. *Learn, if you can, where and how the boys and girls spend their spare time.* That is a good key to character. The seeds of idleness and dissolution are often sown in boyhood at the street corner. Plan, if need be, for the young person's spare time. Be a Big Brother or a Big Sister.

8. *Respect individuality.* Young people are often repressed at home. A deadly error! The boy is not a slave. He is not even a soldier that must accept in silence the command of a superior. Every boy or girl is an individual standing in direct relation to God and responsible to Him. Trust the young people as free men and women. Make them partners with you in whatever you undertake. Be co-workers with them, not their taskmasters.

9. *Encourage the club spirit.* The strength of this spirit is seen in the luxurious growth of the "frat." What is the use of kicking against the pricks of this social instinct? We can control it, but never eradicate it.

10. *Go in for team-work.* Childhood is

selfish; everything centres around the individual. In adolescence the narrow walls of self break down; the world is enlarged. The boy sees that he must work with others. He finds it delightful, too. Help the boy to play the game in a team, thinking not of himself, but of the team. Religious work should also be done in teams wherever possible. Lone tasks are always lonesome. Remember that all this is equally true of girls.

11. Boom athletics. If you cannot have an athletic club in the society, find out what clubs the members belong to, and visit them. Most societies can get up teams, however, and play intersociety matches.

12. Emphasize the practical value of religion. Show that religion is an asset in life. No employer wants an irreligious, unprincipled employee. Religion means character, worth, respect in the community.

13. Make the church lovable. The Intermediate should feel that the church is his home. How to produce this feeling is another matter; but it has been done, and can be done again.

14. Magnify the ministry. There is a decline, we are told, in the number of students for the ministry. Young men take to engineering, law, medicine, everything but theology. Why? Is it because these professions pay more? Possibly this may influence some people in their choice, but not all. One trouble is that young people are not given a vision of the opportunity to make their lives count in really great and abiding work as ministers of Jesus Christ. Think of Dr. Grenfell. If he had become a successful doctor in a thriving city, could his work compare with the work he is doing in Labrador?

15. *Make religion positive.* Let it be the joyous doing of joyous tasks, and not the negative refraining from things that one would like to do if one dared.

16. *Relate religion to life*, to the boy's life or the girl's life. "Did you ever hear the like?" cried an old deacon concerning a minister who was striking at particular sins. "Who ever heard of religion having to do with private conduct?" Through concrete cases show how religion grips into home life, business life, all life. As the cross on the spires of ancient cathedrals towered above the market-place where men bought and sold, so let the young people feel that all life is consecrated by the presence of the living Christ.

17. *Encourage hero-worship.* Every boy is a potential hero. He loves heroes because he feels that he is one himself—in his dreams. Give biography a chief place in the society.

18. *Develop unselfishness.* Remember that this is at bottom an unselfish age. Young people are chivalrous, and chivalry should be

made one of their ideals. In a few years the chance for these lessons will be past. Let each Intermediate follow the simple rule of trying to do one kind act each day.

19. Plan Bible-study. This is a hard task, and calls for wisdom. Perhaps as good a plan as any is to follow a course of Bible-study under a competent leader. If the Sunday-school is giving such a course, let the Intermediates follow it, giving them points for efficiency.

20. Encourage socials. In spite of the attempt to keep the sexes apart they gravitate together. It is human nature. Calf love is frequently caused by a boy's not being brought into contact under proper conditions with girls of his own age. Socials afford opportunity for female companionship, and this is the right of every healthy boy.

21. Work with the pastor. He should be the counsellor of the Intermediate society. Suggestions should be sought from him, and the society should stand ready to do the tasks that he thinks ought to be done. The Intermediates should all be pastor's aids.

22. Set up hard tasks. The heroic age demands them. If the work is easy or insignificant, it will not appeal to boys and girls that are testing their strength. The tasks should not be impossible of accomplishment, but neither should they be too slight.

23. *Let the society be self-governing.* Make it a miniature republic. Let the Intermediates appoint a court for discipline. They should make their own laws and enforce them. This is fine training in citizenship and the use of liberty.

24. *Coach the leader of the meeting.* The Intermediate is in training; therefore he needs help. Assist him to plan his programme; make suggestions to him, and help him to carry them out.

25. *Encourage the timid in the meeting.* A nod of the head or a kindly smile reassures a beginner who is timid and faltering. The approval of the superintendent means much. Never lose an opportunity to speak a word of encouragement to one that has made an effort to take part in a meeting, no matter how slight the part may have been.

26. *Have a prayer circle in a separate room five minutes before the meeting.* Let the leader, the president of the society, and a few of the most earnest workers be present, and as many as care to come.

27. *Have a surprise in every meeting.* Take pains to plan for this, and always be on the lookout for new ideas.

28. *Find out what books the Intermediates read, and then study them.* Talk about these books in the meeting, and suggest others.

29. *Keep a note-book* for the double purpose of catching ideas and plans as they come to you, and for writing down any information that may come to you from any of the members.

30. *Plan business meetings* with the president and committee meetings with the chairmen of committees.

CHAPTER VI

ORGANIZATION

1. Where to Organize

THE ideal place to organize an Intermediate society is a church where there are a goodly number of young people between the ages of thirteen and eighteen, the ideal Intermediate age. Such churches are not so few as one would think. In some instances a canvass of the situation in churches where there does not seem to be abundant youth will show that there is a sufficient number of boys and girls too old for the Junior society and rather young for the Young People's society, that will make splendid material for Intermediate work.

If, however, there are no more than half a dozen available, it is worth while to organize, partly for the sake of the Intermediates themselves, and partly because, if they are rightly directed, they will bring in new members from their acquaintance.

One happy superintendent says: "I began work with the leading members in the church against me. My first meeting was held with only four girls present. I talked to them about their part in Christian work, and we separated

ORGANIZATION

with a promise that we would organize an Intermediate society the next Sunday if each one would bring some one else. We had seven present at the next meeting, and we organized. We have now twenty-seven active members."

Mr. Paul Brown, field secretary of the California Christian Endeavor union, says that the main difference between a Young People's society and an Intermediate society is that the Intermediates are usually more ready to undertake new work and to put more steam into it. If half a dozen young people feel that the society really belongs to them and is not merely run *for* them, they will throw themselves into its plans with a devotion and an enthusiasm that are too often lacking in the older society. One of the strangest objections to the Intermediate society is a very practical one, namely, that it is likely to become so interesting that it will throw the Young People's society into the shade.

To avoid misunderstanding, conflict, and difficulty, the constitution of the Intermediate society should provide for the graduation of Intermediates into the Young People's society at a certain age, eighteen or twenty. This rule should be rigidly adhered to.

Again, when it is proposed to organize an Intermediate society, we are sometimes told that the church is already overorganized.

Sometimes, indeed, this is true. Still, it is possible for a church to take on such a deckload that it becomes top-heavy, while the real cargo lies on the wharf. There are societies that the church cannot afford to do without. If a church had all the organizations under the sky and yet had no prayer-meeting, it would, indeed, be overorganized, but it would not be properly organized. The only thing to do in such circumstances is to make room for the indispensable organization. The fundamental question is not of overorganization, but of the right kind of organization.

Can a church afford to do without a prayer-meeting for boys and girls who are just entering manhood and womanhood? Can it afford to refuse them, or fail to provide for them, an opportunity for training in giving testimony, for public prayer, for expressing their religious life? These things appear vital. The church that neglects them in training its young people will reap a harvest of barrenness in after-years. And nothing can take the place of Christian Endeavor in providing for this kind of practical Christian work. Neither organized Bible class, Knights of King Arthur, Boy Scouts, nor any other organization attempts the kind of work that Christian Endeavor is doing all the time.

If some churches get along without an Intermediate society, why, our fathers got along, too, without electricity, the telephone, the telegraph, and the facilities of modern travel.

We know the advantage of grading classes in secular schools. We even grade the schools themselves. If Intermediate grades are necessary, if trade-schools seem to supply a lack, if institutes, and schools of technology, and universities fulfil a definite purpose, we do not speak of getting along without them or of over-organizing. We simply make room for them. The efficiency of the individual is the important matter, and we must make room for that which vitally affects Christian training.

2. *How to Organize*

Consult the pastor first of all, and secure his hearty consent and promise of co-operation.

Of course the best superintendent available must be found before any public steps are taken. The superintendent and perhaps one or two others interested should give personal invitations to a few of the most promising young people of Intermediate age who are not members of the Christian Endeavor society to meet, preferably, in the home of one of those that give the invitation.

To this small group the subject of Intermediate work should be presented. One might outline a brief talk in this way:

1. The " between " age, when boys and girls

belong neither to the Junior nor the Young People's society. They should have a society of their own.

2. The difference between an Intermediate and a Junior society. The Intermediates have more advanced tasks. Draw an analogy between Christian Endeavor with its graded societies and the public-school system with its graded schools.

3. The difference between the Intermediate and the Young People's society. *a. The age difference.* The Intermediate age is from thirteen (rarely lower) to eighteen or twenty. *b. The difference in having a superintendent.* Intermediates are not supposed to know everything about Christian Endeavor. The superintendent is a trainer, a coach. Draw the analogy between the work of the superintendent and that of a coach.

4. The kind of work Intermediates can do.

5. The field in the church, the chances for getting new members.

6. A description of the Intermediate pledge.

7. Advantages of having a society.

The society may be organized at this first meeting by having those present sign the pledge and appoint officers. Chairmen of committees may be appointed later. A committee should also be appointed to prepare a constitution in consultation with the superintendent.

ORGANIZATION

The superintendent will naturally explain to each officer and committee-chairman the duties of his office. This can be most effectively done in a private conversation.

In preparing for this initial meeting the pastor may announce it from the pulpit, and the Sunday-school superintendent will speak of it in the Sunday-school.

After business has been disposed of have a social hour as a foretaste of the good things that the Intermediates may expect in the society.

3. *The Pledge*

Several forms of the pledge for Intermediates are here given. None of them are binding. Experience, however, has shown that those societies prosper best that keep a high standard of Christian living and duty before the young people in the pledge. For most societies the active member's pledge will be found to meet all requirements.

FORM 1.—ACTIVE MEMBER'S PLEDGE

Trusting in the Lord Jesus Christ for strength, I promise Him that I will strive to do whatever He would like to have me do; that I will pray to Him and read the Bible every day; and that, just so far as I know how, throughout my whole life, I will endeavor to lead a Christian life. As an active member, I promise to be true to all my duties, to be present at, and take some part, aside from singing, in every meeting, unless hindered by some reason which I can conscientiously give to my Lord and Master, Jesus Christ. If obliged to be absent from the monthly consecration-meeting, I will, if possible, send an excuse for absence to the society.

Signed..

REGULAR INTERMEDIATE PLEDGE

Trusting in the Lord Jesus Christ for strength, I promise Him that I will strive to do whatever He would like to have me do ; that I will make it the rule of my life to pray and to read the Bible every day ; that I will attend the services of my own church unless prevented by some reason which I can conscientiously give to my Saviour ; and that just so far as I know how, throughout my whole life, I will endeavor to lead a Christian life.

As an active member, I promise to be true to all my duties, to be present at and to take some part, aside from singing, in every Christian Endeavor prayer-meeting, unless hindered by some reason which I can conscientiously give to my Lord and Master. If obliged to be absent from the monthly consecration-meeting of the society, I will, if possible, send at least a verse of Scripture to be read in response to my name at the roll-call.

Signed..

FORM 3.—ACTIVE MEMBER'S PLEDGE

Trusting in the Lord Jesus Christ for strength, I promise Him that I will strive to do whatever He would have me do. I will make it the rule of my life to pray and read the Bible, to support the work and worship of my church, and to take

ORGANIZATION

my part in the meetings and other activities of this society. I will seek to bring others to Christ, to give as I can for the spread of the Kingdom, to advance my country's welfare, and promote the Christian brotherhood of man. These things I will do unless hindered by conscientious reasons, and in them all I will seek the Saviour's guidance.

Signed............................

FORM 4.—ACTIVE MEMBER'S PLEDGE

Trusting in the Lord Jesus Christ for strength, I promise Him that I will strive to do whatever He would have me do. I will make it the rule of my life to pray and read the Bible, to support the work and worship of my church, and to take my part in the meetings and other activities of this society. These things I will do unless hindered by conscientious reasons, and in them all I will seek the Saviour's guidance.

Signed............................

ASSOCIATE MEMBER'S PLEDGE

As an associate member I promise to attend the prayer-meetings of the society habitually, and declare my willingness to do what I may be called upon to do as an associate member to advance the interests of the society.

Signed............................

4. *The Constitution*

The form of constitution given below is merely a suggestion that may help superintendents in preparing one that will meet their local needs.

Article I.—*Name*

This society shall be called the.......... Intermediate Society of Christian Endeavor.

Article II.—*Object*

Its object shall be to promote an earnest Christian life among its members, to increase their mutual acquaintance, to train them for work in the church, and in every way to make them more useful in the service of God.

Article III.—*Membership*

1. The members shall consist of three classes, active, associate, and affiliated.

2. *Active Members.* The active members of this society shall consist of young persons who believe themselves to be Christians, and who sincerely desire to accomplish the objects above specified. It is left for each society and pastor to determine whether or not active members must be members of the church.

3. *Associate Members.* All young persons of worthy character, who are not at present willing to be considered decided Christians, may become associate members of this society. It is expected that all associate members will habitually attend the prayer-meetings, and that they will in time become active members, and the society will work to this end.

4. *Affiliated Members.* In order to reach and establish a point of contact with young people who for any reason will not join the society,

clubs or classes of any kind, such as civic, athletic, musical, literary, Bible-study, mission-study, and Boys' Brigades, may be organized under the leadership of the Endeavorers, and the members of these clubs shall be accepted as affiliated members of the society. It is hoped that they may soon become active members, and the society will labor to that end.

5. These different persons shall become members upon being elected by the society, after carefully examining the Constitution and upon signing their names to it, thereby pledging themselves to live up to its requirements. Voting power shall be vested in the active members.

6. When Intermediates reach the age of twenty, they shall graduate into the Young People's society.

Article IV.—*Officers*

1. The officers of this society shall be a President, Vice-President, Recording Secretary, Corresponding Secretary, and Treasurer, who shall be chosen from among the active members of the society.[1]

2. There shall also be a Lookout Committee, a Prayer-Meeting Committee, a Missionary Committee, a Social Committee, and such other committees as the needs of each society may require, each consisting of five active members, unless otherwise determined. There shall also

---

[1] If desired, a superintendent may be appointed by the Young People's society, with the approval of the pastor or church, who shall have general charge of the work of the society.

be an Executive Committee, as provided in Article VI.

ARTICLE V.—*Duties of Officers*

1. *President.* The President of the society shall perform the duties usually pertaining to that office. He shall have especial watch over the interests of the society, and it shall be his care to see that the different committees perform the duties devolving upon them. He shall be chairman of the Executive Committee.

2. *Vice-President.* In the absence of the President, the Vice-President shall perform his duties.[1]

3. *Corresponding Secretary.* It shall be the duty of the Corresponding Secretary to keep the local society in communication with the United Society and with the local and State unions, and to present to his own society such matters of interest as may come from the United Society and other authorized sources of Christian Endeavor information. This office should be retained by one person as long as its duties can be efficiently performed, and the name shall be forwarded to the United Society.

4. *Recording Secretary.* It shall be the duty of the Recording Secretary to keep a roll of the members, to correct it from time to time, as may be necessary, and to obtain the signature to the Constitution of each newly elected member; also to correspond with absent members,

---

[1] It is suggested that the Vice-President may also be chairman of the Lookout Committee.

and to inform them of their standing in the society; also to keep correct minutes of all business meetings of the society and of the Executive Committee; also to notify all persons elected to office or to committees, and to do so in writing, if necessary.

5. *Treasurer.* It shall be the duty of the Treasurer to keep safely all money belonging to the society, and to pay out only such sums as shall be voted by the society, or the committees as authorized by the society.

ARTICLE VI.—*Duties of Committees*

1. *Lookout Committee.* It shall be the duty of this committee to bring new members into the society, to introduce them to the work and to the other members, and affectionately to look after and reclaim any that seem indifferent to their duties, as outlined in the pledge. This committee shall also, by personal investigation, satisfy itself of the fitness of young persons to become members of this society, and shall propose their names at least one week before the society votes upon their election.

2. *Prayer-Meeting Committee.* It shall be the duty of this committee to have in charge the prayer-meeting, to see that a topic is assigned and a leader appointed for every meeting, and to do what it can to make the meetings interesting and helpful.

3. *Missionary Committee.* It shall be the duty of this committee to provide for regular missionary meetings, to organize mission-study classes when feasible, to interest the members

of the society in missionary topics, and to aid, in any manner which may seem practicable, the cause of home and foreign missions.

4. *Social Committee.* It shall be the duty of this committee to promote the social interests of the society by welcoming strangers to the meetings, and by providing for the mutual acquaintance of the members by occasional socials, for which any appropriate entertainment, of which the church approves, may be provided.

5. *Executive Committee.*[1] This committee shall consist of the pastor of the church, the officers of the society, the chairmen of the various committees, and the leaders of affiliated groups or clubs. All matters of business requiring debate should be brought first before this committee, and by it reported to the society. Recommendations concerning the finances of the society should also originate with this committee.

6. Each committee, except the Executive, shall make a report in writing to the society, at the monthly business meetings, concerning the work of the past month.

ARTICLE VII.—*The Prayer-Meeting*

All the active members shall attend and heartily support every meeting, unless prevented by some reason which can conscientiously be given to their Master, Jesus Christ.

---

[1] One object of this committee is to prevent waste of time in the regular meetings of the society by useless debate and unnecessary parliamentary practice, which are always harmful to the spirit of a prayer-meeting.

ORGANIZATION

ARTICLE VIII.—*The Pledge*[1]

All persons on becoming active members of the society shall sign the Active Member's Pledge. Associate members shall sign the Associate Member's Pledge.

ARTICLE IX.—*The Consecration-Meeting*

1. *Once each month, or as often as the society may decide, a consecration or covenant meeting may be held, at which the roll may be called, and the responses of the active members shall be considered as renewed expressions of allegiance to Christ. It is expected that if any one is obliged to be absent from this meeting, he will send a message, or at least a verse of Scripture, to be read in response to his name at the roll-call.*[2]

2. If any active member of this society is absent from this meeting, and fails to send a message, the Lookout Committee is expected to take the name of such a one, and in a kind and brotherly spirit ascertain the reason for the absence. *If any active member of the society is absent from three consecutive consecration-meetings, without sending a message, the Lookout Committee and the pastor shall consider the*

---

[1] Samples of various forms in use will be found on another page, from which a selection can be made. If none of these meets the local needs, the pastor and the society are at liberty to formulate a pledge of their own; but it is earnestly hoped that a pledge embracing the ideas of private devotion, loyalty to the church, and outspoken confession of Christ in the weekly meeting will be adopted.

[2] It is recommended that the *first* meeting of each month be observed as consecration-meeting.

matter, and may recommend to the Executive Committee that the member be dropped from the roll.

3. Any associate member who without good reason is regularly absent from the prayer-meetings, and shows no interest whatever in the work of the society, may, upon recommendation of the Lookout Committee and pastor to the Executive Committee, be dropped from the roll of members.

ARTICLE X.—*Relation to the Church*

This society being a part of the church, it shall carry on its work in harmony with the wishes of the official board of the church.

ARTICLE XI.—*Relation to the Junior and Young People's Society*

The Junior society, the Intermediate society, and the Young People's society being united by ties of closest sympathy and common effort, reports should be read from each at the semi-annual meetings of the others. As a rule Junior members attaining the age of fourteen should be graduated into the Intermediate society, and from there at the age of eighteen or twenty into the Young People's society.

ARTICLE XII.—*Fellowship*

This society, while owing allegiance only to its own church and denomination, is united by ties of spiritual fellowship with other Endeavor societies the world around. This fellowship is based upon a common love to Christ, the principles of a common covenant, and common methods of work, and is guaranteed by a common name, "Christian Endeavor," used either alone or in connection with some denominational name.

This fellowship is that of an interdenominational, not an undenominational, organization. It is promoted by local-union meetings, State and national conventions, and in many other ways.

Article XIII.— *Withdrawals*

Any member who may wish to withdraw from the society shall state the reasons to the Lookout Committee and pastor. On their recommendation to the Executive Committee, the member's name may be dropped from the roll.

Article XIV.—*Expansion*

Any other committees may be added and duties assumed by this society which in the future may seem best.

Article XV.—*Amendment*

This Constitution may be amended at any regular business meeting by a two-thirds vote of the entire active membership of the society, provided that a written statement of the proposed amendment shall have been read to the society and deposited with the Secretary at the regular business-meeting next preceding.

Specimen By-Laws[1]

Article I

This society shall hold a prayer-meeting on the .... evening of each week. The first regular prayer-meeting of the month shall be a consecration-meeting, at which the roll shall be called.

Article II

Method of Conducting the Consecration-Meeting

At this meeting the roll may be called by the leader during the meeting or at its close. After the opening exercises the names of five or more may be called, and then a hymn may be sung or a prayer offered. The committees may be called by themselves, the letters of the alphabet merely may be called (all whose names begin with A responding first, etc.), or other variations of the roll-call may be introduced. Thus varied, with singing and prayer interspersed, the entire roll shall be called. During the meeting, or at its close, the list of associate members may be called, the associates answering, "Present."

Article III

This society may hold its regular business-meeting[2] in connection with the .... regu-

---

[1] If it is thought that these rules and regulations are unnecessarily long, it should be borne distinctly in mind that these specimen By-Laws are simply given as *suggestions*.

[2] This business-meeting will usually be simply for the hearing of reports from the committees, or for such matters as will not detract from the spiritual tone of the meeting.

lar prayer-meeting in the month, or in connection with a monthly social. Special business-meetings may be held at the call of the President.

Article IV

The election of officers and committees shall be held at the first business-meeting in . . . . . .

A Nominating Committee shall be appointed by the President at least two weeks previous to the time for electing new officers. Of this committee the pastor shall be a member *ex officio*. If the society so orders, the officers and committee chairmen only may be elected, the new Executive Committee filling out the committees. It is understood that these officers are chosen subject to the approval of the church. If there is no objection on the part of the church, the election stands.

Article V

Applications for membership may be made on printed forms, which shall be supplied by the Lookout Committee and returned to them for consideration.

Names may be proposed for membership one week before the business-meeting, and shall be voted on by the society at that meeting.[1]

Article VI

Persons who have forfeited their membership may be readmitted on recommendation of the

---

[1] It is recommended that the new members be formally received at the consecration-meeting following their election.

Lookout Committee and pastor, and by vote of the members present at any regular business meeting.

Article VII

New members shall sign the Constitution within four weeks from their election, to confirm the vote of the society.

Article VIII

Letters of introduction to other Christian Endeavor societies shall be given to members *in good standing* who apply to be released from their obligations to the society, this release to take effect when they shall become members of another society; until then, their names shall be kept on the absent list. Members removing to other places, or desiring to join other Christian Endeavor societies in the same city or town, are requested to obtain letters of introduction within six months from the time of their leaving, unless they shall give satisfactory reasons to the society for their further delay.

Article IX

Other committees may be added, according to the needs of the society, of which the following are examples:

Information Committee. It shall be the duty of this committee to gather interesting and helpful information concerning Endeavorers or Endeavor work in all parts of the world, and to report the same. For this purpose five minutes

ORGANIZATION 69

shall be set aside at the beginning of each meeting.

Sunday-School Committee. It shall be the duty of this committee to endeavor to bring into the Sunday-school those who do not attend elsewhere, and to co-operate with the superintendent and officers of the school in all ways that they may suggest for the benefit of the Sunday-school.

Calling Committee. It shall be the duty of this committee to have a special care for those among the young people that do not feel at home in the church, to call on them, and to remind others where calls should be made.

Music Committee. It shall be the duty of this committee to provide for the singing at the young people's meeting, and also to turn the musical ability of the society to account when the Endeavorers can be helpful at public religious meetings.

Flower Committee. It shall be the duty of this committee to provide flowers for the pulpit, and to distribute them to the sick at the close of the Sabbath services.

Temperance Committee. It shall be the duty of this committee to do what may be deemed best to promote temperance principles and sentiment among the members of the society.

Relief Committee. It shall be the duty of this committee to do what it can to cheer and aid, by material comforts, if possible and necessary, the sick and destitute among the young people of the church and Sunday-school.

Good-Literature Committee. It shall be the duty of this committee to do its utmost to promote the reading of good books and papers. To this end, it shall do what it can to circulate among its members *The Christian Endeavor World,* also to obtain subscribers for the denominational papers and missionary magazines among the families of the congregation as the pastor and church may direct. It may, if deemed best, distribute tracts and religious leaflets, and introduce good reading-matter in any other suitable way which may be desired.

Press Committee. It shall be the duty of this committee to send items regarding the work of the society and church to the newspapers accessible to it, and in all feasible ways to use for Christ the power of printers' ink.

The Whatsoever Committee. This committee shall consist of graduates from the Junior society,—all boys, if the society maintains also a Lend-a-Hand Committee. The Junior superintendent or some other older person shall be chairman of the committee, and its members shall aid the other committees in doing their work, take up the little duties that do not fall to the lot of any other committee, and in this way obtain an introduction to the work of the older society.

The Lend-a-Hand Committee. This committee, if it is formed, shall consist of the girl graduates from the Junior society, and its work shall be similar to that of the Whatsoever Committee.

Other committees not here found may be

added as occasion may demand and the church may desire.[1]

Article X

Members that cannot meet with this society for a time are requested to obtain leave of absence, which shall be granted by the society and withdrawn at any time, on recommendation of the Lookout Committee and the pastor, and their names shall be placed on the absent list.

Article XI

.... members shall constitute a quorum.

Article XII

These By-Laws may be amended by a two-thirds vote of the members present at any regular meeting, provided that notice of such amendment is read to the society, and given in writing to the Secretary at least one week before the amendment is acted upon.

---

[1] Many societies find it a good plan to have so many committees that every member may serve on a committee or hold an office, thus receiving definite training by service.

CHAPTER VII

HOW TO MAKE SUCCESSFUL MEETINGS

Rev. Charles Stelzle tells a good story about two young men from the East Side in New York. Said the one, "Mawruss, what do them letters mean, D. D., M. D., LL. D. ?"

"They mean brains," replied Mawruss with emphasis. "D. D. means Doctor of Divinity; M. D. means Doctor of Medicine; and LL. D. means Doctor of Laws."

A week or two afterward Mawruss met his friend again, and the young man pulled out a visiting-card, and handed it to him. On the card was the name, and, trailing after it, the cryptic letters "FF, FF, F."

"What do these letters mean?" inquired Mawruss. "FF, FF, F. What does it mean?"

"Dat means brains," answered his friend.

"Yes, but how brains?" persisted Mawruss. "FF, FF, F."

"Dat means two fires, two failures, and one fortune."

To make a prayer-meeting successful requires brains. The superintendent that thinks that societies run themselves, or that success is won without effort, will make more than two failures.

If we think meanly of the Intermediate society, we shall have poor, uninteresting meetings. But if we think largely about the society, and plan for large and important things, we are on the highroad to success.

Remember that Intermediates will follow the line of their deepest interests. Look at the road that leads to a baseball-field when a big game is on. It is black with people. They are interested, and their interest draws them. So we must study the Intermediates, just as the advertisement-writer studies men and what appeals to men. The young man's interest must be made the point of contact. If superintendents asked themselves what the young people are interested in, what will appeal most strongly to them, we should hear of less failure. We must distinguish between our own interests and the interests of boys and girls in their teens.

Too little attention is paid to the accessories of the meetings. Here are a few hints:

1. Make the room attractive. The object in getting young people to attend meetings is not to make them gloomy martyrs.

2. Look to the lighting. A half-dark room is a poor place to hold a meeting. Young people like brightness for most meetings. Of course some prayer-meetings may be held in a dim light.

3. Have good seats. No one likes to be uncomfortable.

4. Ventilation is important. The reason why people yawn in street-cars, for example, is because the air is vitiated, deoxygenized. People fall asleep in church for the same reason.

5. The temperature should be right. Too much heat or cold should be avoided.

6. Give a good deal of thought to the music. A good leader is an absolute necessity. Spirited singing is one of the best attractions for young people.

7. Make large use of the blackboard. If there is a member with any talent for drawing, make him the society artist. Of course, others may assist him. Arrange to have at least one point illustrated by a blackboard drawing at every meeting.

Preparation for the Meeting

It goes without saying that the superintendent must prepare for the meeting, not only by much prayer, but also by a careful study of the topic. He should outline some simple methods and suggest them, if necessary, to the leader of the meeting in a private talk with him a week in advance.

Every member should read the daily readings. Urge the Intermediates to keep a note-book at hand and write down each day one thought that strikes them. If they read over their notes before the meeting, they will have more than sufficient material for a short talk.

A good plan is to take a month's or a three months' pledge to read the daily readings every day, write out one thought daily, and give at least one original thought in the meeting.

How Conduct the Meetings?

"It is my conviction," writes Mr. Paul Brown, field secretary of the California Christian Endeavor union, "that the Intermediate society should be conducted on almost the same lines that were originally laid down for the Young People's society, and that the older societies should tackle some advance work and methods."

This expresses the consensus of opinion among Intermediate workers, with this difference, however, that there must be more variety in the Intermediate meeting than in the Young People's. Thus, Intermediates enjoy meetings that have special features such as a leaderless meeting, a chairless meeting, when each member receives a chair as he or she takes part, a meeting with the chairs arranged in a circle or in the shape of the Christian Endeavor monogram, and so forth.

"Our little society of thirty members," writes a correspondent from California, "is not yet a year old, but it has had a wonderful influence, especially among the boys. We have had a splendid superintendent, a high-school teacher, who is constantly in touch with young people. Our ages run from fourteen to twenty-one years.

"We have established a little prayer circle before the meeting. Often six or eight members take part. There has been very little trouble about slip-reading, since all seem to be willing to develop a question or give a long article in their own words. The subject is given them on the Monday or Tuesday before the Sunday on which it is to be reported.

"The meetings are usually started with a few songs, and then the repetition of the Lord's Prayer seems to give tone to the meeting. We have decorated our rather bare room with green burlap screens and with flowers."

Giving to the Intermediates questions in writing with the request that they answer them in the meeting has been worked successfully in many societies. There are many that will write out their replies and read them who could not take part in any other way. In other societies fifteen minutes of each meeting are given to reading some interesting book, and this works well when the books are well chosen. The Intermediates may take turns, if this is practicable, in reading.

The helps printed for the Young People's societies in *The Christian Endeavor World*

SUCCESSFUL MEETINGS

should be used for the Intermediate society adapted, if need be, to local conditions.

Different Kinds of Meetings

The list of such meetings is limited only by the ingenuity of the superintendent or members. A few suggestions will show what can be done.

1. A leaderless meeting. The programme is written on the blackboard, and is followed closely. Some societies have timed each item. The president of one society intimated that when the time came for general participation, and an interval of thirty seconds elapsed during which no one took part, he would close the meeting.

2. A chairless meeting. As each one takes part, he is given a chair, and takes his seat.

3. A monogram meeting, the chairs being arranged in the form of the Christian Endeavor monogram. On a wet night it gives a cozy impression to have the chairs arranged in a circle. They may be arranged in the shape of a fan, or a cross, and so on.

4. A solo meeting, when nothing is done in concert, but every part of the programme is carried out by a single individual. Solos should also be sung, of course.

5. A duet meeting, when the chairs are arranged in pairs. When one member of a pair rises to take part, the other member must also rise and take part. The Scripture lesson should also be read by having each couple take a verse. Duets are in order.

6. *A trio meeting* is carried out in the same way as a duet meeting, but everything must be done in threes.

7. *An inverted meeting.* The leader conducts this meeting from the back of the room.

8. *A divided meeting*, the girls being seated on one side of the room and the boys on the other. This meeting may be worked as a contest between boys and girls, or they may simply take part alternately.

9. *A quartette meeting*, in which a quartette of boys or girls lead, and all that is done is done by four people acting at once where this is possible, or one after the other.

10. *A favorite-hymn meeting*, each member selecting a hymn beforehand and giving it out in the meeting, at the same time telling one or two facts about the hymn or the author.

11. *A memory meeting.* No books are used in this meeting. Instead of reading the Scriptures let the members quote from memory their favorite verses. Hymns may be sung from memory, too.

12. *Absent members' meeting.* Letters from absent members should be read. In securing these letters tell the absent members what the

topic is, and ask them to answer definite questions.

13. Post-office meeting. The members write letters on the topic to the president, and hand them to him before the meeting. Two or three members may read these letters during the meeting.

14. A sealed-order meeting. In this case the president or secretary gives to each member as he enters the room a slip of paper with a request on it to do some special thing during the meeting, to engage in prayer, to take part, to announce a hymn, and so forth. The success of this meeting lies, of course, in the willingness of every one to do what he is told.

15. A biographical meeting. The members will each come prepared to tell some of the main facts about some life that has inspired them. A brief biography of the authors of the hymns sung should also be given.

16. Question-box meetings. At the close of one meeting a question-box should be opened, and the members should be requested to put questions into it. At the next meeting another opportunity for questions should be given. The pastor or some experienced worker should reply to the questions, giving the members an opportunity to express themselves if they desire. A good plan is to have workers present to answer questions that may fall under their speciality. Thus the pastor will naturally take Bible questions; the Sunday-school superintendent will take questions relating to Sunday-school work, and so on.

17. *An information meeting.* In this meeting each member is expected to give one fact about Christian Endeavor. It is well to divide the theme, assigning to some to speak about Christian Endeavor history; to others, about Christian Endeavor principles; to others, Christian Endeavor methods; and to yet others, Christian Endeavor achievements. Such a meeting convinces some Endeavorers that they do not know all that they ought to know about Christian Endeavor, and spurs them to study.

18. *A vacation meeting.* At the beginning of the season it is well to have the Intermediates tell of their experiences during the summer. If the superintendent will write out a few questions and hand them to different members, he will broaden the scope of the meeting and bring out helpful ideas.

19. *An object meeting.* To this meeting each member is asked to bring some object and to draw one helpful lesson from it. In this case there will, of course, be a great variety of objects. A similar meeting may be narrowed down to a flower meeting, a nature meeting, or something like that.

20. *A church-echo meeting.* The members

may be asked to attend church in the forenoon, and make notes of the best part of the sermon. At the meeting they will give it in their own words, telling how it impressed them. If the words of a hymn have impressed one, of course he will tell of that.

21. A Bible-promise meeting. The members may be asked to find some of the great promises of the Bible and repeat them in the meeting, adding a few words of their own. Others will tell how the promises of God are sure, and others, how they have been fulfilled. Some will probably tell of promises fulfilled in their own experience.

22. A beginners' meeting. This will be a fine opportunity to get near the beginners and encourage them to do something, however little. An older member may be assigned to each beginner to help him, to suggest what he should say, and to sit beside him during the meeting. Very often the beginner will follow or precede this older member, strengthened by his interest and presence.

23. A chain meeting. As each one takes part, he is permitted to call on some one else to follow him. This means that each one must come prepared to do something.

24. A pleasant-memory meeting. The members are asked to come prepared to relate one pleasant memory. Letters from absent members, from church officers, and from friends, may be secured and used in the meeting.

25. *A candle-light meeting.* Sometimes the members are supplied with candles; and, as each person takes part, he lights his candle from the leader's candle, which stands in the centre of the table. With this method, however, clothes are liable to be damaged by grease; so other ways have been devised. One society had a large wooden cross prepared. In the wood were bored a large number of holes the size of the end of a candle. The members were given candles; and, as each took part, he went to the front, where the cross lay on the floor, lighted his candle, and placed it in one of the holes. The effect was very fine. Another society used a board with the holes arranged in the shape of the Christian Endeavor monogram.

26. *A young men's meeting.* A special meeting may be held for the young men, to which the boys bring their friends. A programme that touches young men's interests should be prepared in advance, and nothing should be left to chance. Plan everything carefully and well.

27. *A young women's meeting* may be held on the same day as the young men's meeting, if desired, but in a different room. At the close of the meetings a united praise service lasting ten minutes might be conducted.

28. A standing meeting. The members stand at the back of the hall; and, as each one takes part, he walks to the front and takes his seat.

29. A staff meeting. On single-track railroads the engineer of a train was at one time given a staff by the station-master to show that the track was clear and to indicate that he had right of way. In the staff meeting a staff (a roll of cardboard will do, or a Bible) is passed from one member to another, the one receiving the staff having right of way, and taking part before he hands the staff to another.

30. A cottage prayer-meeting. Hold the meeting once in a while in different surroundings, the home of one of the members, the room of a shut-in, or in some institute or home. The programme should be prepared in advance.

31. A sunrise meeting, held at the same hour in the morning as the meeting is usually held at night, is attractive once in a while. An added attraction is a breakfast served in the church parlors after the meeting.

32. A suggestion meeting in which the members are expected not only to criticise the society, but to suggest one way to better it, or to outline some work that it might undertake.

33. A song meeting is always attractive. The songs of one author may be used, and the story connected with each may be told. Variations of this are a meeting for gospel songs, or for songs written in the Middle Ages, each prefaced with a brief account of the author's life. Or songs written in one century may be chosen, or songs of the Scottish Covenanters, or songs of the Reformation, and so on.

34. A carnation meeting. Each member is given a carnation as he comes into the hall. Some societies prefer to hand out the flowers as the members take part.

35. A fathers' meeting. Some of the boys may not care to take prominent part in this meeting; so the programme should be arranged to give the fathers an inning. If the superintendent will get in touch with a number of the boys' fathers and assign to them subjects on which he wishes them to speak, the meeting will be a success. Special invitations should be sent to the fathers, of course.

CHAPTER VIII

BIBLE DRILLS

ONE important difference between the Young People's meeting and that of the Intermediates is the use of Bible drills in the latter. Perhaps there is as much need of such drills in the one place as the other, for there is a woful lack of knowledge of the Bible even among mature Christians. It is not uncommon to see people looking for the book of Revelation in the Old Testament, or the book of Judges in the New.

The Intermediate society provides an excellent opportunity for the Intermediates to make themselves acquainted with the books of the Bible. It is practice that counts in this, as in everything else. Much of the knowledge that we laboriously acquire in school is lost later in life, because we have not been called upon to use it. Who can name offhand the capitals of the less conspicuous countries in Europe, Bosnia, Croatia, and even Denmark? In the Junior society the boys and girls often learn how to find the books of the Bible, but they forget if they do not keep at it. The Intermediate society furnishes excellent practice.

Besides, Bible drills may be carried much

farther in the Intermediate society than is possible in the Junior, because the intelligence of the members is more developed. We can get Intermediates to memorize Bible verses that have a definite relation to one another. Thus we can take a Bible topic and pursue it in a Bible drill that will fix it in the mind. What would some of us not give to have been taught great texts dealing with great topics in this way? Woodrow Wilson remarks: "It is very difficult for a man, for a boy, who knows the Scriptures ever to get away from it. It haunts him like an old song. It follows him like the memory of his mother. It reminds him like the word of an old and revered teacher. It forms part of the warp and woof of his life."

In carrying on Bible drills use the blackboard, and get the Intermediates to copy the outline of the day's drill in a note-book kept for this purpose alone.

Suppose we begin with the books of the Bible. We write on the blackboard the total number, sixty-six. We point out that these books were written by different authors at different periods of history; that each book unfolds some special aspect of God's revelation of Himself, the later books, generally speaking, attaining greater and greater clearness, until the Old Testament revelation bursts into flower in God's revelation of Himself in His Son, Jesus Christ. Then this revelation is expanded and expounded in the books of the New Testament.

To help Intermediates to memorize the names of the books of the Bible and to form a clear mental picture of their positions in the Book, write out on the blackboard a scheme like the following :

Historical Books	*Poetical Books*	*Prophetical Books*
Genesis	Job	Isaiah
Exodus	Psalms	Jeremiah
Leviticus	Proverbs	Lamentations
Numbers	Ecclesiastes	Ezekiel
Deuteronomy	Song of Solomon	Daniel
Joshua		Hosea
Judges		Joel
Ruth		Amos
1 and 2 Samuel		Obadiah
1 and 2 Kings		Jonah
1 and 2 Chronicles		Micah
Ezra		Nahum
Nehemiah		Habakkuk
Esther		Zephaniah
		Haggai
		Zechariah
		Malachi

The very names of the books suggest the divisions to which they belong; and, as these divisions follow one another, the general position of each book is easily determined.

But look at the divisions a little more closely. The first five books in the first division are called the Pentateuch, and contain the story of the creation, the history of the patriarchs, the exodus of the children of Israel from Egypt, and their journey to Canaan. The last book is a summary of the law and the circumstances attending the giving of it. It is essential that the Intermediates know not only the names of the books, but also the general contents.

After Israel entered Canaan, and Moses had passed away, a new leader arose, Joshua. His work is related in the book that bears his name. After Joshua came the Judges, who ruled Israel before the people demanded a king, and the book of Judges tells us of their exploits. The beautiful idyl of Ruth follows the book of Judges, because it belongs to that historical period. And after Ruth comes Samuel, the last of the judges. Samuel's successors were Saul the king, and David, both anointed by him. Hence the books of Kings follow Samuel. The books of Chronicles retell the story of the kings of Israel and Judah from a religious and hortatory standpoint.

The history related in these books carries us to the Babylonish captivity, when the entire nation was deported to Babylon. Ezra and Nehemiah were among those that returned from Babylon to Canaan, and their books record the events that led up to the return. The patriotic story related in the book of Esther tells of an incident of the dark years of the captivity.

When the connection between the books is presented in this way, it is no longer a hard task to find them.

The poetical books will not present any difficulty. They, too, follow the historical order. Job is, of course, the oldest, and stands first. The Psalms, many of them the work of David, comes next. Then Proverbs and Ecclesiastes, both attributed to Solomon, the son of David.

Turning to the prophets, we find that there are four large books which, for this reason, have been called the major prophets. They are arranged in their historical order also. Isaiah comes first; then Jeremiah, who lived during the events that led up to the captivity; then Ezekiel, who lived during the captivity and prophesied in Babylon; and Daniel, whose story is well known. Merely to call attention to this relation fixes the position of these books.

Then follow twelve minor prophets helter-skelter, without order of any kind. These twelve names must simply be memorized and worked over until they find a permanent place in the mind.

The books of the New Testament may be dealt with in the same way under four heads, Gospels, History, Epistles, and Prophecy.

From Matthew to Corinthians the way is clear. From this point the Intermediates should take the books in groups, thus:

> Galatians
> Ephesians
> Philippians
> Colossians

Then come the five T's: the two epistles to the Thessalonians, the two letters to Timothy, and the letter to Titus. After Titus we have Paul's last personal epistle, that to Philemon. Then comes the letter to the Hebrews. After this come the writings of other apostles: Peter's two letters; John's three letters; the epistle by Jude; and the Revelation.

Knowledge of the position of the books of the Bible should be constantly tested by verse drills. The superintendent should call chapter and verse, and finally the name of a book, and let the members see how quickly they can find the place. A spell-down of this kind is sure to create interest, and it should be frequently held.

The Books of the Bible

Beginning with the books of the New Testament, Intermediates will find that the books of the Bible form a series of fascinating studies. The blackboard should be used for outlines. One superintendent writes that her Intermediates commenced with the Gospels, and used the following outline for each, giving fifteen minutes to the drill.

1. Number of chapters.
2. Author's name and character.
3. Where the book was written.
4. When the book was written.

5. Why the book was written.
6. For whom the book was written.
7. Jesus described as—(in the case of Matthew, for example, the word "Messiah" would be inserted here).
8. Emphatic truth.
9. What is especially recorded.
10. Characteristics.
11. Frequent expressions.
12. Key-word.
13. Key-verse.
14. Favorite verses.
15. Conclusion.

This sort of drill should be a blessing, not only to Intermediates, but also to superintendents. It will help to keep their Bible knowledge fresh; and, if they lack knowledge, will drive them to obtain it by careful study. A good plan is to secure a reliable commentary on the book to be studied, and to read it along with the Bible. Care, however, must be taken, in this case, to keep out technical discussions and stick to simple truths.

A Palestine Drill

The superintendent above referred to introduced a study of Palestine under the headings given below:

1. The provinces of Palestine and the length of time spent by Christ in each.
2. The homes of Jesus, their distance and direction from Jerusalem.

3. Mountains connected with the life of Christ.

4. Principal bodies of water mentioned in the New Testament.

This might be largely extended. For example, a study of Jerusalem itself might be made, which would give a fine opportunity to refer to ancient customs.

In the same way missionary drills may be prepared, which will give the members a new idea of missions.

Alphabet Drill

Intermediates are not beyond making a Bible alphabet of their own. The simplest form of this is to ask the members to find and memorize texts beginning with a certain letter of the alphabet; the letter A the first week; B, the second week; C, the third; and so on. Each Intermediate keeps a record of the texts he has memorized; and, when the alphabet is finished, an examination may be held in the shape of a spell-down to see who has remembered the texts memorized.

A variation is to assign to each Intermediate a different letter of the alphabet with the request that he find a text beginning with this letter. In this way the whole alphabet is gone over in one meeting. The next Sunday different letters are assigned.

A Book-Knowledge Contest

Divide the society into two parts, taking care to have the sides fairly evenly matched. Appoint a captain for each side, and assign a book of the Bible—a book chosen from the New Testament is best to begin with—to be studied by all. After two weeks' or a month's study, as the case may be, have a contest between the sides to see which has attained the more accurate knowledge of the contents of the book.

To conduct the contest a referee should be appointed, the pastor, perhaps, or the superintendent himself. The referee will determine whether a question is allowable or not, and will settle any matter in dispute. His decision is final. A judge may be appointed besides the referee.

The two sides stand facing each other. The captains alternately put questions, based on the contents of the book under study, to the opposite side, beginning with the first person in the opposing row. If he cannot answer the question put to him, this person takes his seat, and the same question is put to number two, and so on until it is answered. The side that puts out all their opponents is the winner.

Study Drill

Give the Intermediates two or three weeks to read through a book of the New Testament.

say one of the Gospels. Ask them, as they read, to supply to each chapter a short title which will suggest to them the main contents of the chapter. At the time appointed the Intermediates will bring this list of titles to the meeting and read it—in the following manner:

Each one will read the title he suggests for the first chapter. Then the members will be asked to name the best title suggested for this chapter. If there is a difference of opinion, vote on the matter. When the best title has been fixed upon, write it on the blackboard and let the Intermediates copy it. In this way go through the entire list of chapters.

Each member will then have this revised list. Give a week now to memorize it. Thereafter, week by week, drill the members on the contents of the various chapters. A question like "What are the contents of St. Matthew, chapter ten?" should bring out a correct reply at once. By taking book by book the members will soon gain a working knowledge of the contents, and, better than that, will know how to go to work to make out lists of their own.

The titles of the chapters must be very brief. They are not meant to cover the contents of each chapter, but to suggest them. A few from Matthew will show what is intended.

The Gospel by Matthew:

Chapter 1. Genealogy, through Joseph.
" 2. Birth of Jesus.
" 3. The Baptist.
" 4. Temptation.
" 5, 6, and 7. Sermon on the Mount.
" 8. Miracles.
" 9. More miracles.
" 10. Call of the twelve.
" 11. John's question.
" 12. Controversy.
" 13. Parables of the Kingdom.
" 14. Herod and John.
" 15. Rebuke to Pharisees.
" 16. The great confession.
" 17. Transfiguration.
" 18. The child-text.
" 19. Discussion in Judea.
" 20. The shadow of death.
" 21. Entry into Jerusalem.
" 22. Herodians, Sadducees, and Pharisees.
" 23. Marks of a Pharisee.
" 24. Jesus' prophecy.
" 25. Parables of the return.
" 26. Conspiracy against Jesus.
" 27. Delivered to death.
" 28. Resurrection.

Topic Drill

Occasional drills in the study of Bible topics should be introduced for the purpose of teaching the members how to handle their Bibles. There is no better book of helps for preparing such drills than Professor Wells's work, "The Bible Marksman," published by the United Society of Christian Endeavor, Tremont Temple, Boston, Mass., price, thirty-five cents, post-paid.

A sample drill will give an idea of the way these topics are treated.

The subject is "Christ," and the subtopics are:

1. Prophecies of Christ (Isa. 53 : 4–12).
2. His divinity (John 1 : 1–5, 18, 34).
3. His character (Heb. 12 : 2).
4. His mission (Matt. 20 : 28).
5. His authority (Phil. 2, 9, 11).
6. His love (John 15 : 9–15).
7. His atonement (John 3 : 14, 15).

Under each head are given a number of Scripture texts which throw light upon the topic. Thus:

1. Prophecies of Christ. Gen. 3 : 15 ; 12 : 3 ; 49 : 10 ; Num. 24 : 17 ; Deut. 18 : 15 ; Job 19 : 25 ; Ps. 2 : 6–9 ; 22 : 18 ; 69 : 7–9, 21 ; 72 : 2–17 ; 110 : 1 ; Isa. 9 : 6, 7 ; 11 : 1–10 ; 32 : 2 ; 40 : 9–11 ; 42 : 1–7 ; 52 : 13, 14 ; 61 : 1–3 ; 63 : 1–9 ; Jer. 23 : 5, 6 ; Ezek. 34 : 23 ; Dan. 2 : 35, 44 ; 7 : 13, 14 ; Mic. 5 : 2 ; Zech. 9 : 9, 10 ; 13 : 1 ; Mal. 3 : 1–3 ; 4 : 2.

2. His divinity. Matt. 12 : 41, 42 ; 26 : 63, 64 ; Luke 22 : 70 ; 24 : 25–27 ; John 5 : 17, 18, 23 ; 6 : 54, 62 ; 8 : 23, 28, 56–58 ; 10 : 30–38 ; 13 : 19 ; 14 : 6, 11, 19 ; 17 : 5 ; 2 Cor. 5 : 19 ; Col. 2 : 9.

BIBLE DRILLS

In this fashion each of the seven subtopics is expanded.

The Intermediates should be taught how to use a Bible concordance, how by this means to trace a subject in the Scriptures and weave text into text. The advantage of drills like this is not merely that they impart knowledge, but that they teach the young people to think for themselves, and show them how to enter upon individual research. The blessing of God rests upon him who knows how to search the Scriptures intelligently.

Bible Text-Matches

Sides are chosen with a captain on each side. Then Scripture texts are repeated, first by one side, then by the other, and any one that fails to give a text in his turn sits down. The side that keeps up longest wins.

Bible Arches

A Philadelphia superintendent has been teaching his Intermediates Bible history with the help of a blackboard on which he drew eight arches, each representing a period.

Around the outside of the first arch the names of the Bible characters that lived during that period are written. One name is given to each Intermediate (eight or ten Intermediates being used) a week in advance, and he tells the life-story of the individual assigned to him. Inside the arch are written the principal events of the period.

Thus, around the first arch appear the names Adam, Eve, Cain, Abel, Seth, Jared, Enoch. Inside the arch, the following events: creation of the world; fall of man; death of Abel; translation of Enoch.

Each Old Testament arch is supposed to cover one thousand years; each New Testament arch, twenty-five years. Beginning the second millennium, therefore, with the name Methuselah, we end with Abraham; and the events are: wickedness of the world; the flood; the tower of Babel.

The third arch begins with Isaac, and takes in the great names in history up to and including the time of Solomon, covering also events like the journeys of the patriarchs, the sojourn in Egypt, the wilderness, the conquest of Canaan, the judges, and the rule of the kings. The fourth period stretches from Elijah to Christ, and the events are: the capture of the tribes; Babylonian captivity; and the return of the Jews. Constant reviews keep the names and events of each period fresh in mind.

CHAPTER IX[1]

COMMITTEES AT WORK

THE PRAYER-MEETING COMMITTEE

THE superintendent should attend every meeting of the prayer-meeting committee, one of the most important in the society. He should encourage the members to plan the meetings, making suggestions only when absolutely necessary. The scope of the committee's activity is the same as in the Young People's society, so that all the helps suitable for that society may easily be adapted to Intermediate work. The members should be encouraged to scan the pages of *The Christian Endeavor World* for such helps, and to make use of that paper in preparing for any given topic.

The committee will, of course, prepare topic-cards, and see that every member gets one. This is a small item, but it gives individuality to a society to have its own cards, and the members appreciate it.

---

[1] When any piece of work suggested in this or succeeding chapters seems to duplicate work done by the Young People's society, the superintendent should arrange with the Young People's society so that duplication may be avoided. For instance, the flower committees of the Young People's and Intermediate societies should supplement each other rather than conflict in their work.

Again, the committee will appoint leaders, and the members will stand ready to lead the meeting, should a leader fail to appear. A society copy of *The Christian Endeavor World* is a necessity, and the chairman of the prayer-meeting committee should see that this copy is placed in the hands of the leaders well in advance of the meeting.

Planning the Meetings

Every meeting should contain a surprise, and should be different, in some respect, from the previous meeting. If the committee members are supplied with Professor Wells's book, "Prayer-Meeting Methods," which may be secured from the United Society of Christian Endeavor, Tremont Temple, Boston, Mass., for thirty-five cents, there will be no dearth of ideas for novel and interesting meetings.

A superintendent in California says that they have arranged some novel meetings, each different from the other. Here is the list:

A Jack-o'-lantern meeting in which a great Christian Endeavor monogram in red and white, the Christian Endeavor colors, was used. This lantern was used again on the Fourth of July with the addition of some blue stars on the white background.

A convention meeting for the benefit of those that could not attend the State convention.

PRAYER-MEETING COMMITTEE 101

This meeting was held during the time of the convention, and the music and talks and every part of the meeting carried out, as far as possible, the convention spirit.

A wire meeting, at which ten-word telegrams were written to the pastor, who was on his vacation, to the ruling elder of the church, and to members who had been absent from three consecutive meetings.

A shower meeting, at which each member was asked to give at least five favorite Bible verses, each participant being followed immediately by another. Songs about showers were sung, and a shower of gifts for a children's hospital was presented.

A pause meeting, in which pauses were conspicuous by their absence. A well-equipped pause committee, appointed several weeks before the meeting, helped to make this meeting successful.

A special sing, the sole purpose of which was to give an opportunity to sing to their hearts' content. A good opportunity to make the acquaintance of new hymns.

A debate meeting, the subject, home and foreign missions, being treated by two well-prepared sides. Much information was gained by the society as to the needs of both fields.

A motto meeting for the purpose of calling attention to the mottoes of the United Society of

Christian Endeavor, the State union, the county union, and the city union.

A work meeting was held at the beginning of the school year. The pure joy of hard work was emphasized, and especially the joy of working for Christ.

Many other novel meetings may be arranged to correspond with the topic, as, for example, a printer's meeting, for the topic, "Reading That Is Worth While." Of course the regular Christian Endeavor topic is always used, and these subtitles are used simply to prevent stereotyped meetings and to arouse curiosity as to just what will be done at the meeting.

A gramophone meeting in another society proved a great success. Records of gospel hymns were used. An enterprising leader secured from the Victor Gramophone Company, Camden, N. J., a record of a short speech made by Dr. Francis E. Clark, and used it at their meeting.

Work with the Members

The efficient prayer-meeting committee will find a large field of work among the members. On it rests the responsibility of getting the members to take part in the meeting. Some superintendents have no difficulty in getting the girls to participate, but fail to make the boys break silence. Others, again, maintain that the young people of both sexes are quite as ready to take part in the meeting as are the members of the Young People's society. Probably the same problems must be faced in both societies.

How shall we attack this problem in the Intermediate society? One superintendent replies that he has solved it by giving to the members questions to be answered in the meeting. Another finds that an informal discussion of the topic yields better results than short talks, and far more express their opinions in this way. Still another finds that sentence prayers following the treatment of the topic help many to break down the fears of the members, for the topic has aroused some thought or other which they can express in a single sentence in the form of a desire.

A pause committee, suggested above, may set a good example by filling in pauses that are likely to kill a meeting. A very efficient society appointed a timekeeper to see how much time was lost by the members' not taking part promptly, and not coming to the meeting on time. At the end of the first month the timekeeper reported that, while only a few minutes had been lost because of pauses during the meeting, more than eight hours in the aggregate had been lost by members' coming late.

The members of the prayer-meeting committee may assign among themselves the names of younger and timid Intermediates, so that each member of the committee becomes responsible for one or two of them. He will visit those assigned to him, encourage them to take part, suggest simple things that they may do, and help them to do these. He can begin by giving a timid member a clipping and ask him to read it. After this has been done a few times he may suggest that the clipping be memorized and spoken. After this has grown more or less familiar it may be suggested that the member master the thought contained in the clipping, and give the thought in his own words. It will then be easy to get the member to read a verse of Scripture and add just a single sentence of his own, or to take part in a sentence prayer.

The superintendent should have a well-marked plan like the above to suggest to the members of the prayer-meeting committee for their personal work among the members. At the committee meetings reports of progress should be made. A committee that really gets down to business in this way is sure to succeed, and the effect of its work will be felt in the society.

A Purpose Card

Distribute among the members a card like the following:

"*I Am Willing*

"To offer prayer in the Christian Endeavor meeting if called upon.

"To join in sentence prayers.

"As a rule, to add something of my own, if only a sentence, to what I may read in the meeting.

"To lead a meeting.

"To lead a meeting along with some one else.

"I wish to become a Comrade of the Quiet Hour.

"Let the members check off the points that express their willingness, and hand the cards to the president."

These cards might well be distributed every three months, and the members may be urged to take new responsibilities upon them, since growth is the law of life.

A Standard

In the ideal society, which, of course, does not exist, even if it ought to, every member would be prepared to take part in every meeting, adding something of his own in addition to a verse of Scripture or to a clipping read, if such are used.

Every member, moreover, would be a Comrade of the Quiet Hour, since the strength of a society may be measured by the depth of the members' spiritual life, and this can best be fed by private devotion.

Again, every member would be willing to lead the meeting either alone or together with some one else.

And at the consecration-meeting each one would answer at roll-call, or send a greeting if obliged to be absent. These meetings would always vary, and the method of calling the roll would rarely be twice alike.

In the ideal society the members would encourage the weaker and younger members to take part; no one would ever be criticised, and no one would ever feel ashamed.

Furthermore, in the ideal society the prayer-meeting committee will meet with the leaders and help them to plan their meetings. This need not take so much time as would appear necessary. It means that one hour a month should be given to the work. All the leaders for the coming month will attend this meeting, and their meetings will be planned one after the other.

Sermon Reports

Interest will be aroused if the committee appoints each week three or four members of the society to report just one thought from the pastor's Sunday-morning sermon. This thought will not always be in keeping with the topic, of course, but the duty of reporting something will exercise the judgment of the reporters and give them practice in expressing their thought.

Prayer Circles

This committee should take the lead in organizing prayer circles wherever possible. Each circle should consist of about three members, and the membership of circles should not be made public. One or two circles are enough to start with. The circles meet for prayer for definite objects, and they keep on praying until the answer comes. Some circles keep a prayer calendar, praying for certain members of the society, or for outsiders whom they wish to draw into Christian Endeavor fellowship. When it seems likely to help, new members are asked to join the circles; but, when a circle doubles its membership, it usually divides into two, and the process of growth begins again. These circles have been a great blessing in Californian societies.

Pre-Prayer Service

The pre-prayer service is a prayer-meeting held in an adjoining room five minutes before the hour of the regular prayer-meeting, and it is open to all. The prayer-meeting committee will, of course, be present, the leader of the meeting, and others that are interested. This brief moment of communion with God, when all take part, each in a brief prayer, is often a source of strength and blessing.

CHAPTER X

COMMITTEES AT WORK

The Lookout Committee

The Intermediate society should prepare its members for graduation into the Young People's society by training them in committee work similar to that followed in the older society. The chairman of each committee should have a committee scrap-book, the property of the committee, in whose pages he should write or paste any suggestive plans that he comes across. He should also possess—indeed, the society should furnish him with—a copy of some book or leaflet dealing with the work of his committee. It is a good plan to let both scrap-book and other committee helps circulate among the members, so that all may be interested in suggesting new plans, and all may gain a clear idea of what is expected of the committee. The United Society of Christian Endeavor issues helps of all kinds for committee work.

The superintendent will, of course, supervise the committee work, making sure that the chairmen understand what is expected of them. Some committees will be able, after a while, to work more or less alone; but others will need careful attention all the time. For example, the prayer-meeting committee. Good prayer-meetings do not happen. They must be planned. It is true that the Intermediates will do a prodigious amount of planning, but there are times when they need help and wise suggestions. The superintendent should attend all the committee meetings that this committee holds, ready to help in any way. This holds true of the important committees like the lookout committee, the missionary, and so on.

The Lookout Committee

This committee should always be alert to bring in new members. Some suggestions as to methods employed may be helpful.

An Invitation

A card of invitation urging young people to attend the Intermediate society may be prepared and distributed by the members among friends, in church, in Sunday-school, and elsewhere.

Personal Invitations

The lookout committee may survey the ground and make a list of names of possible new members. One or two of these names are then assigned to each committee member, who is requested to call on the young people and report back to the committee at its next meeting. Some societies use a report-card which is filled out and returned at once to the chairman of the committee. The card reads:

"Will you kindly try to bring John Doe, 15 Tremont Street, to the Intermediate society? As soon as you have tried will you kindly report on the back of this card, and hand it to me?
"(Signed)   JAMES JONES,
"*Chairman of the Lookout Committee.*"

Where these cards are used, the chairman assigns the names of those he wishes visited, and reports are made at once instead of waiting until the next committee meeting.

SEALED ORDERS

The committee may enlist the help of every member in the society in securing new members. This has the advantage of increasing interest by increasing the number of workers. At the regular meeting of the society every member is given a sealed envelope containing the name of some one whom the member is asked to visit and invite to the meeting. A report-card similar to the one above given may be supplied, along with the name of the person to be visited.

At the next meeting similar envelopes are

given out containing the same names, which, however, are given to different members. Thus John Doe, let us say, is invited by A to attend the Intermediate meeting. Next week he is invited by B. The third week he also receives an invitation, this time from C, and so on. This plan, which persistently keeps at prospective members, often results in their joining the society. A great many people wait until they are asked to join, you know.

Membership Contests

The simplest form of contest is to divide the society into two sides, the reds and the blues, and let each side strive to win as many members as possible. A contest for membership alone, however, is hardly worth while. The important matter is not to get new names on the roll, but new people to attend the meetings. So attendance should be added to membership, and points given for that. Thus points may be given somewhat in this fashion:

For each new member	10 points
For each visitor	2 "
For each member present	1 point
For each member taking part in prayer	2 points
For each member taking part by speaking	2 "
For each member reading an extract from book or paper	1 point

LOOKOUT COMMITTEE 113

As each member takes part, the captain of his side will make a record of the fact, and place the number of points gained opposite the name of that member. At the end of three months, or whatever time is agreed upon, the total points won by each side is counted, and the losers give the winners a banquet.

This programme can be varied in endless ways.

In one society each member was supplied with a card on which he kept his own record for each month. On the card were printed the items for which credits were given, and the number of credits for each; and opposite each item were five spaces in which the member wrote the number of points gained each week. From these cards the secretary of the society reckoned the count of each side.

One society divided into two sides, and then each side subdivided itself into squads of five. Each squad worked for new members; and, when one was gained, he was added to the squad that introduced him.

Another variation of this contest plan is a trip to Japan or any other country. The items and their credits are first of all made out. Then the distance, in miles, to Japan, or to the destination of the society, is fixed. The society has of course been divided into two companies, each with a name; and the contest is to see which covers the distance first, one credit counting one mile.

Both on sea and land travellers are liable to be wrecked. So wrecks may be introduced into this contest. For example, a rule may be made to the effect that, if one of the sides has fewer members present at a given meeting than were present at the previous meeting, this shall be considered a wreck, and a number of credits corresponding to the number of absent members shall be subtracted from the record of that side.

Some have applied this principle to an aëroplane race, adding interest by having a model aëroplane, decorated with the side's colors, for each side. A race between an aëroplane and a balloon is sure to interest.

In membership contests the sides have been organized as "searching parties." They may be scouts or anything that will appeal to the imagination of the young people.

It is a good rule to insist that all persons wishing to join the society attend at least four consecutive meetings before their application for membership is considered. Intermediates will take the society at the superintendent's valuation. If he magnifies it, they will do so, too. A rule of this kind, rigidly enforced, will surely result in a good attendance.

Church-Attendance Contest

A live society had a contest to see which side could get most people to come to church. The Intermediates not only came themselves, but brought hosts of friends and acquaintances. Each person invited by an Intermediate counted one point, provided they attended the church service. Children under twelve didn't count, however.

Old Folks' Day

If an Old Folks' Day be tried one year, it will become an institution. The members specially invite those old people that can come to church unaided, while carriages or automobiles are hired or borrowed for those that are unable to walk. It is astonishing how many owners of automobiles will gladly lend them for such a time as this.

In the Hotels

The Intermediates can offer their services to the pastor or church officers to distribute cards in hotels, boarding-houses, railroad depots, and so forth, inviting travellers, lodgers, visitors, everybody, to come to the church services. The lookout committee may also take the lead in a survey of the church or district if the pastor wishes such work done. Every member of the society will surely stand ready to help.

The Stranger

The lookout committee is not only on duty at the Intermediate meeting. It can be on the lookout for new members at church. It can keep watch for newcomers and be ready with a hearty invitation to attend the Intermediate society.

Associate Members

The lookout committee should constantly seek to increase the list of associate members, and to see that these members are approached, at least once a year, if not oftener, and urged to enter active membership. The associates should be put on committees such as the flower committee, pastor's aid, information, good-literature, citizenship, temperance, and missionary.

Personal Work

The Intermediates may be organized into personal workers' bands for the study of evangelism, for training, consultation, and for prayer. Not all will join this band; but some will, and they will become the best workers. Intermediates will do personal evangelistic work in their own effective way, and they are not too young to be taught how to lead souls to Christ.

LOOKOUT COMMITTEE

Keeping a Record

Whenever a record of attendance or of the participation of the members in the meeting is to be kept (and both will be kept in every well-regulated society), the work is in charge of the lookout committee. In the case of a contest, of course, the record will be kept by the two sides. Some societies have found it inspiring to keep a record of the attendance of Intermediates at church and at the midweek prayer-meeting, reporting the number for each week at the end of the month.

The Midweek Meeting

The lookout committee may divide the society into four parts, and assign to each band one church prayer-meeting to attend in the month. In this way the entire society serves once a month.

Contest for a Christian Endeavor Pin

This contest, tried in a Chicago society, for an Intermediate Christian Endeavor pin, will give an idea as to how points for such a contest may be arranged. The contest opened May 1, and closed in the middle of June. Longer time, of course, may be given to it. All regular attenders were privileged to try, and the person that secured the largest number of marks won the pin.

Attendance at each regular meeting of
   the society - - - - -   5 points
Attendance at each social or business
   meeting - - - - -   5   "
Bringing a new visitor, eligible for
   membership, to the Sunday meeting 10 "
Reading Matthew - - - 10 "
         Mark - - -   10 "
         Luke - - - - 10 "
         John - - - - 10 "
         Acts - - - - 10 "
         Heroes of Modern Missions
            (Chipman) - - - 10 "
         Men of Mark in Modern Missions (Grose) - - - 10 "
         Servants of the King (Speer) 15 "
         Stewardship and Missions
            (Cook) - - - 15 "
         Any other missionary book,
            150 pages or more - - 15 "

Holding Members

It is quite as important to hold members as it is to win them, and this work also falls to the lookout committee.

The lookout committee should have a secretary as well as a chairman. The duty of the secretary is to keep a record of absentees, for waning interest is usually marked by absence from the regular meeting of the society. If the lookout secretary keeps a special roll for the use of this committee, marking the attendance every week, he will be able to tell at a glance what members need the attention of the committee.

The secretary will then distribute the names of absentees among the members of the committee, asking the members to call on the individuals whose names have been handed to them.

A visit to the home of an Intermediate means not a little, and a kindly personal invitation to attend the regular meeting is often effectual. A good deal of tact must be used on such visits, and the most tactful members of the society should be placed on this committee.

When a visit is not possible, a special written invitation to attend the next meeting of the society is the next best thing to do. In such cases be sparing with rebukes. Remember the words of the apostle Paul, " Love never faileth."

CHAPTER XI

COMMITTEES AT WORK

The Missionary Committee

The chairman of the missionary committee must be constantly reminded to keep in touch with the missionary board of his denomination and ask for whatever helps and suggestions for the topics are published. Since a successful missionary meeting requires not only careful planning, but also careful preparation, each meeting should be planned at least a month in advance. The members of the committee must study the topic themselves and be ready to take part, and they must do their utmost to get others to promise to participate in the meeting, suggesting things that each may do.

Mission Study

The committee will do well to organize a mission-study class, using as a text-book one of the many volumes issued for this purpose. The first thing to do is to secure a teacher for the class. For Intermediates the very best teacher procurable should be secured. Perhaps the pastor may undertake the work; if not, he may be able to suggest a good leader. Or the local

MISSIONARY COMMITTEE

Christian Endeavor union may be able to supply one.

The members of the committee should form the nucleus of the class, and each member ought to try to bring another with him. A class of ten is a good size. The more Intermediates that can be brought into such classes, the more interest will there be in missionary work, and the better will be the missionary meetings.

Missionary Giving

Since people support only causes that appeal to them, the best way to increase the missionary offerings of the society is to disseminate information on missionary topics; and the mission-study class is one way of doing this effectually. It has been proved many times that, when a society has a definite object toward which its money goes, it is comparatively easy to secure the funds. Thus some societies have undertaken to support an orphan in some mission land, or to support a student at some mission school, or to pay part of the salary of some worker. In these cases regular reports from the field are made to the society, which is thus continually kept in touch.

Again, a missionary-reading contest is likely to increase interest in missions and so swell missionary receipts. A small prize may be given to the member that reads and reports intelligently on the largest number of missionary books in a given time. The size of the books should be taken into consideration, of course. Prizes should not be very valuable, or envy may result.

It has been found helpful for the society to fix, at the beginning of the financial year, a definite sum which it will give to home and foreign missions; then for the committee to plan for the raising of this amount in a systematic manner. Perhaps the very best way to raise missionary money is to adopt the envelope system. Small gifts regularly made very soon mount up.

The responsibilities of stewardship ought to be emphasized by the missionary committee, since training in missionary giving is an essential part of a young person's Christian education. Pledges may be taken from the members to cover the expenses of the society and for missions, and duplex envelopes may be used for this purpose. Here is a card that has done good service in a Chicago society:

"For the work of the Intermediate society of Christian Endeavor of the Third Congregational Church, Oak Park, Ill., for the current year I will contribute
.... cents each week for current expenses, and
.... cents each week for benefactions.

"It is understood that this pledge becomes void for the balance of the year in case of my removal, or in case of my putting into the hands of the superintendent a written notice of cancellation.

"Name..

"Street no...........................

"Date......................."

The two sides of the duplex envelope read as follows:

"Let every one of you (*individually*) lay by him in store on the first day of the week (*systematically*) as God hath prospered him (*proportionately*)."—1 Cor. 16 : 2.	"Bring an offering, and come into his courts."— Ps. 96 : 8.
Current Expenses *Intermediate Society of* *Christian Endeavor* *Third Congregational Church* *Oak Park, Ill.*	*Benefactions* *for* *The Extension of the* *Kingdom*
$	$ . . . .
This side for ourselves.	This side for others.

The left-hand side is printed in black, the right-hand side in red.

Missionary Plans

The Intermediates should be led to study the mission fields of their denomination and to pray for the missionaries in these and other fields. The Chicago society above referred to publishes quarterly for its members a prayer calendar in connection with its prayer-meeting topics. A brief example will show how the calendar is arranged. The first topic of the quarter is "Missions in China," and the topic suggested for prayer for the first Sunday is "Chicago's Representatives in China." Then follows:

"*North China Mission*
"Monday, Sept. 4. Mrs. Mary P. Ament, Pekin. Work for Women. 1877.
Miss Isabelle Phelps, Pao-ting-fu. Evangelistic work. 1910.
Tuesday, Sept. 5. Miss Jessie E. Payne, Pekin. Principal of girls' boarding-school. 1904.
Miss Mary H. Porter, Pekin. Principal of women's training-school. 1868."

In this way the workers in this North China mission are gone over one by one, after which the workers in the Shansi mission, the Foochow mission, and the South China mission, are mentioned, the date when each worker entered upon his or her field being given, and the kind of work in which they are engaged.

Then missions in India are taken up in the same way, then Turkey, and so on. In this way the Intermediates, who engage each day to remember these workers in prayer, are made familiar with the names of the missionaries and with their work. A prayer calendar may be arranged by the superintendent, or by the missionary committee with his aid, from the list of missionaries that each denomination will gladly provide.

Missionary Meetings

The simplest kind of missionary meeting is to have the missionary committee study the topic and assign to each one a two-minute talk on some aspect of it. Besides this, have the committee prepare a set of questions to which replies must be made in figures, such as the population of the country under discussion, the year when the first missionary went forth, the number of church-members, the number of heathen, and so forth. At the meeting slips with these numbers written on them are distributed among the audience.

After the usual exercises the leader may open with a brief talk. He may ask a question of one committee member, who in answering it will give his talk. The leader may then put a question to the audience, calling for a reply in numbers; and he will then ask whoever thinks he has the proper answer on his slip to read it. This makes everybody take notice. Mistakes and quaint guesses at the right answer will be made. Then other members of the committee will take part, and opportunity will be given to all the Intermediates to participate. A few questions, distributed a week beforehand, will be found helpful in suggesting topics for others to study and speak on.

A Sale of Pearls

A touch of color may be introduced occasionally if some of those that take part are in costume. One society tried a sale of pearls. A member, dressed as a Buddhist, entered, and tried to sell to one of his audience the pearl of Buddhism. He explained the system, bringing out its good points, while the one whom he addressed raised objections from the Christian standpoint. Then came a Mohammedan with his pearl, and representatives of the various heathen religions. Finally came a Christian with the pearl of great price, which was adjudged worthy of purchase.

Different Kinds of Meetings

1. A missionary debate. Two teams should be appointed to conduct this, each team under a captain.

2. A missionary camp-fire, as realistic as possible. Electric bulbs, covered with red paper and placed under a few fagots, will make an excellent imitation of a fire. The

MISSIONARY COMMITTEE 127

meeting must be planned beforehand, and each member should have a "gun" to fire.

3. An extract meeting, at which the members give extracts from the works or letters of missionaries, or recount their experiences.

4. A memorial meeting in honor of missionary martyrs cannot fail to interest Intermediates. To make it successful, assign the name of a martyred missionary to each member, and tell him or her where to find an account of the missionary's life. Each member will relate very briefly the story of his hero and draw one impressive lesson from his life.

5. A camera meeting, at which pictures of mission fields and work are shown in connection with brief talks. Each member should, of course, be asked to bring a picture. The missionary magazines supply a plenty.

6. A medical meeting, when the work of medical missionaries is described. The field is very wide, and there is no lack of material for such a meeting. Assign to different members the various fields, and suggest books to read on the topic.

7. A missionary quiz is an excellent way to impart knowledge. A list of questions should be prepared dealing with every phase of missionary work, about missionary countries, the number of inhabitants in them, about the various religions, about the missionary boards engaged

in the various fields, about great missionaries, about the missionaries of the denomination, about missionary giving, and so on. The replies to these questions may be written on slips of paper and distributed among the members. As the questions are asked by the leader, each member will, of course, be forced to keep in mind the reply on his slip to see whether it fits the query.

8. A missionary-newspaper meeting. Two editors are appointed a month or more in advance of this meeting. They make out a table of contents for the paper they wish to get out, and secure contributions in accordance with this plan from the members of the society. Suppose the topic is Japan, the contents of the newspaper might be as follows: Two editorials; Ancient Japan; When Christ First Came to Japan; The New Era in Japan; What Missions Have Done for Japan; Neesima; Japan To-day; Things I Saw in Japan; Missions in Japan; Search-lights (brief paragraphs about Japan and missions); a poem. At the meeting the editors may ask the authors each to read their own compositions, or may read them themselves, turn about.

Schemes for missionary meetings are simply endless, and this dullest of meetings may be made bright by means of a little thought. One might have a missionary biography meeting, a meeting that would describe the work of women

MISSIONARY COMMITTEE

in mission fields, a miracle meeting that would tell the thrilling story of the conversion of heathen tribes, an impersonation meeting, when the speakers would appear in costume, a missionary news-box, a question-box, and so on.

Whenever possible, secure the services of a returned missionary to address the Intermediates. Almost everywhere in cities Student Volunteers are to be found who are eager to address missionary gatherings. They are young men ready themselves to go to the mission field, and they are sure to impart some of their enthusiasm to Intermediates.

Each member of the missionary committee should keep a scrap-book, and never lose an opportunity to write in, or paste in, new missionary plans. The members should also have books like "The Missionary Manual," by Professor Amos R. Wells, and "Fuel for Missionary Fires," by Belle M. Brain, both published by the United Society of Christian Endeavor, Tremont Temple, Boston, Mass. Use should also be made of the missionary exercises issued by the United Society at ten cents each.

A prize consisting of a Christian Endeavor book or a Christian Endeavor pin offered for the best essay on a given missionary topic, the society to be judge, or, if the number of essays is too great, the missionary committee or the pastor to judge which is best, will supply a fresh impulse.

The missionary committee may make itself felt not only on nights when the missionary topics are studied, but all through the month, by organizing as an information committee and giving at least one missionary item at each meeting of the society.

If each member will promise to collect as many cents as he is years old, and give this amount for missions on his birthday, a nice little sum will be realized.

The missionary meeting will be brightened if the committee collect pictures and curios from mission lands and have a missionary exhibition bearing on the topic.

Try a club of Intermediates, each member of which promises to read a missionary book for fifteen minutes each day for a month.

Finally, devise new plans yourself. Have something new at every meeting, and the missionary meeting will be the best of all meetings.

CHAPTER XII

COMMITTEES AT WORK

THE SOCIAL COMMITTEE

CHRISTIAN ENDEAVOR aims at the development of the whole boy or girl, and not of a part of his or her nature. The Intermediate prayer-meeting will take care of the religious instincts, and the work outlined in committees will provide that activity and usefulness for which every young person craves; but something must be done for the awakening social instinct, which often finds satisfaction in dance-hall or party.

Some leaders of thought, especially in rural districts, are urging the addition of a play-hour to the Sunday-school service. Where it has been tried, the attendance has materially increased, and better order is maintained in the Sunday-school because those that misbehave are punished by being excluded from the games following. Whatever may be thought of this on the Sabbath-day (and it will certainly rasp in the minds of many), the idea of conducting play-hours under the leadership of the church is a good one. Such hours need not, of course, fall on Sunday at all.

A society in New York, which has its regular Christian Endeavor meeting on Sunday evenings, has a weekly social on Friday nights, which attracts many young people and their friends, besides strangers. A social every week may seem too much, but under proper leadership it might prove a great boon to Intermediates. Elaborate preparations need not be made for every social; a simple programme of singing and clean games is enough. It is time that the church took a hand in the social life of its young people, and the Intermediate society provides a starting-point.

The social committee must be supplied with books that describe games and social entertainments. Professor Wells's book, "Social to Save," and another little volume entitled "Eighty Pleasant Evenings," both published by the United Society of Christian Endeavor, Tremont Temple, Boston, Mass., at thirty-five cents each, contain material for many a successful social. The committee members should keep scrap-books, and carefully watch the pages of *The Christian Endeavor World*, *The Ladies' Home Journal*, and other papers, for plans for practical socials. The superintendent will try to be present at every meeting of the social committee, and plans adopted in his absence should be submitted to him for his approval and for suggestions.

A Bell Social

Cards inviting to this social should be cut in the shape of bells, and should announce that both bells and belles are wanted at a certain time and place. Each person attending should be requested to bring a bell—any kind of bell—electric bell, cow-bell, hand-bell, alarm-bell, large or small bell. At the social each bell must tell its experience, its uses, and suggest a lesson. Songs and music should be connected in some way with bells; and, if cake or ice-cream is served, the bell shape is appropriate.

A Police Social

The invitation is a summons, and contains the information that a policeman will be sent to fetch every one that will not come voluntarily. At the door the guests are met by a police officer who escorts them into the cloak-room, where witty signs adorn the walls. Then the friendly policeman ushers the guests into a large hall where notices are posted in conspicuous places. "Keep off the grass." On the wood-box, "To be used in case of fire." On the ceiling, a big red sign, "Any one staring at the ceiling will be committed to the asylum." When one stops in front of the sign reading,

"Notice. Do not look at this sign," a policeman pounces upon him, and hales him off to be tried. The judge severely questions the accused, who is obliged to defend his own case. The guilty are made to stand in the rogues' gallery and listen to the flattering remarks of sightseers.

Advertising Social

Each one that comes to this social is expected to advertise his or her business. The guests are asked beforehand to personate representatives of various trades and professions. Lawyers, doctors, preachers, artists, bookkeepers, smiths, mechanics, salesgirls, housewives, and so forth, talk up their work, using all the wit and ingenuity of which they are capable to make out a good case.

Old-Time Social

An old-time social should be held in costume; and, if real costumes cannot be procured, imitation dresses may be made from paper. Old-time poems should be read, old-time songs sung; and everything should be done in the style of bygone days, including the courtly manners of our forefathers. Historical charades and tableaux may be introduced. A good old-fashioned spelling-bee will be in place.

Handkerchief-Bazaar

An Oklahoma society made $250 by means of a handkerchief-bazaar. The invitations were a rhymed announcement of the bazaar and its purpose, and the closing stanza read:

> " So this, then, is our plea in brief:
> To aid our enterprise
> We beg of you a handkerchief
> Of any kind or size."

A shoal of handkerchiefs came in and were sold at the bazaar.

An Athletic "Meet"

The guests at a Nebraska society's social were all tagged with small college emblems. There were six emblems, a small paper football, an oar, a baseball bat, a pennant, a tennis-racket, and a running-shoe. These separated the company into groups, all those with the same emblem holding together.

The programme was a thirty-inch dash, hammer-throw, shot-put, standing broad grin, and relay race.

For each of the first four events each college was requested to send out three representatives; for the last event the winners of the former events were chosen.

For the thirty-inch dash pieces of string thirty inches long, with a luscious marshmallow attached to the end, were prepared. The free end of the strings was placed between the teeth of the contestants, who were required to race for the marshmallow, using only lips and teeth. Judges kept record.

For the hammer-throw a paper bag was inflated and tied with a string, the teams trying to throw it as far as possible. The shot-put meant that each contestant was to drop ten beans into quart jars ranged along the floor. The participants toed a line and threw the beans into the jars. After this the "standing broad grin was easy." The grins were measured, and the broadest won.

The relay race was run by the groups of victors. Each group was ranged in a row, each member being provided with a dry soda-cracker. At a given signal the first man in each group began to eat his cracker. When he finished, he held up his hand and opened his mouth, and number two in his group began, and so on.

The winners of all events were announced through a megaphone, and a shaving-mug was given to one of them instead of a loving-cup.

SOAP-BUBBLE CONTESTS

A soap-bubble party, described in the *New York Tribune*, affords no end of fun, and is suitable for any time of the year, as it can be held either indoors or outdoors.

SOCIAL COMMITTEE

Clay pipes gayly decorated with ribbons, two of a color, determine partners. To the large bowl of soapy water add a tablespoonful of glycerine to give beauty of color. The larger your bubbles grow, the more lovely are the tints.

Competition may take many forms, and rewards, of course, must be given to the most successful. Bouquets of flowers make suitable awards.

For "bubble croquet" have a table covered with a woollen cloth, and have ribbon-wound wickets placed in the right order. Sides are taken and each player may blow three bubbles at a turn, guiding them through the wickets with the aid of small rackets, the kind used for pingpong. Cover the wider part with flannel or some thin woollen goods. Bubbles will not break easily against woollen. Rackets may be made of palm-leaf fans cut the required shape and covered with the woollen fabric. It counts five points every time a bubble is guided through a wicket.

Another game is played on a tennis-court. For indoors divide off the room into sides by a rope or ribbon stretched across. The girls make bubbles, and the boys try to blow them over the net, trying also to prevent those of their opponents from coming over into their domain. Each bubble that floats over the net counts fifteen points to the side from which it came.

Then there are trials of skill. For these you will need a few extra articles—a funnel, a straw, a rose or other flower, and a goblet. Place the rose on a large pie-plate. Dip your pipe into the bubble water; and, as you take it out, hold it over the top of the rose and blow until the flower is covered with the bubble; then lift up your pipe, carefully place the funnel on top of the bubble, and continue blowing. Blow very carefully, and the result will be a rose under an exquisite dome. A bubble like this will last at least ten minutes.

Blow a good-sized bubble on top of a goblet, insert carefully in the side a straw that has been dipped in the solution, and blow off a tiny bubble. You can fill the whole interior of the big bubble with these small ones that keep floating around the inside.

Another trick with the help of a straw is to decorate each finger-tip with a bubble. Dip the five fingers into the solution and a drop of it will adhere to each one. Place the wet end of the straw against each drop in turn and blow gently. The result will be a bubble on each finger-tip.

Hold a flower in your hand by its stem, and blow a bubble over it with the pipe. The sunflower makes a fine show, and the blower should be congratulated on his skill, as it takes a big bubble to cover it.

Cupid's Archery

Cupid's archery contest was a winner at a Brooklyn social on Valentine's Day.

Six white hearts were attached to a large red heart. The white hearts contained the following inscriptions: 1, Matrimonial Success; 2, Despair; 3, Hope; 4, A Proposal; 5, Five Times Wedded; 6, Bachelorhood or Spinsterhood.

Each player was given a paper arrow with a pin at the point. The player was then blindfolded, turned in the direction of the heart, and asked to jab it with his arrow. One can imagine the fun that this created among the two hundred young people present.

The social opened with a debate, after which the Endeavorers searched for the five hundred and fifty hearts that were hidden in every nook and corner of the room. There were two hundred red hearts, which counted five points each to the finders; three hundred white hearts, which counted one point each; and fifty candy hearts, the value and sweetness of which were found in the eating. A prize was given to the one that made the most points.

A romance in song was another winning feature. A blackboard was placed in front of the piano. On the blackboard questions were written, and the audience guessed the answers, which were woven into melodies played by the pianist.

Successful Socials

To handle a crowd of young people there must be a live leader, whose main effort must be to get the crowd into good humor and make everybody acquainted. A social at which a young man, for instance, is allowed to sit a silent spectator, or to stand in a corner, taking no part in the fun, does positive damage to him. When it is over, he will go home bitter at heart because nobody drew him out, and perhaps be mad at himself for being such a fool as not to mix with the others. The social committee must be impressed with the idea that their first and most important duty is to root out wallflowers, male and female, and break up all stiffness.

A hundred schemes may be worked to break the ice and set people talking and laughing. One way is to distribute a number of picture puzzles and tell the guests to find the other parts of the pictures. Sometimes each guest wears a tag with his or her name; pencils and cards are provided for each; and the people are told that a prize will be given to the one that speaks to and secures the signature of the greatest number of guests within a given time. **The prize** must be some ludicrous trifle, of course. At one social the guests were arranged in two rows facing each other. To the end man of each row was given a plate of peanuts (the same number in each plate), and at a certain signal the peanuts were passed along the row from hand to hand, one at a time, to see which side could handle them most expeditiously.

A peanut-race is always enjoyed. The runners carry each a peanut on the point of a knife. If the nut is dropped, it must be picked up with the knife alone.

Sometimes the plans for a social harmonize so that everything fits into the character of the social; but at other times it is necessary to have fillers, little games or stunts to create fun. Here are a few suggestions.

An obstacle-race. At the starting-line the contestants must thread a needle. Then they run to a chair in the centre of the room, where they pick up a dry soda-cracker and eat it. Then off to another chair at the other end of the room, where they drink a glass of water. Then back to the starting-point.

A nail-driving contest for girls, each being given a certain number of nails and a hammer; a wool-winding contest for boys, using the left hand; a skipping-rope for boys; a poem parodying a popular song and making local allusions (which must be good-natured and harmless);

a telegram contest, ten letters being written on the blackboard for the guests to use as the initial letters of a ten-word telegram, the funnier, the better.

In handling a large company a contest is a good idea. Divide the company into two parts on any principle desired. Thus, foreigners may be seated on one side of the hall and Americans on the other; or Easterners may sit on the one side and Westerners on the other. This done, wheel the blackboard, which should be prepared beforehand, into place, and the contest opens. Suppose we have an authors' contest. Write the following sentences on the blackboard, and ask the sides to solve them, one at a time. The side that solves the larger number correctly wins.

1. What you get when you fall into the fire. (*Burns.*)
2. What is meat doing in the oven? (*Browning.*)
3. What the Pilgrim Fathers came to this country to establish. (*Holmes.*)
4. A great spiritual ruler. (*Pope.*)
5. What women sometimes wear on their heads. (*Hood.*)
6. A worker in precious metals. (*Goldsmith.*)
7. What nobody wants on his foot. (*Bunyan.*)
8. The seat of the emotions. (*Harte.*)

Professor Wells makes the following suggestions for good socials, which may serve as seed thoughts:

A garden party, the social being held out-of-doors.

A soap-bubble social, with contests in blowing the bubbles.

A polar social, devoted to the elucidation of explorations in arctic and antarctic regions—especially timely.

An indoor picnic, with decorations that make it seem as much outdoors as possible.

A railroad social, the chairs arranged as in a car, the exercises referring to railroads.

A social held at some private house, where the Endeavorers are forced to get closer together.

A State social, whose exercises recall the famous men and events of your State history.

A botanical social, the chief feature of which is a contest in naming the leaves of various kinds of trees, branches of which are stuck into vases.

A fagot party, each participant being given a small fagot, during the burning of which he must tell a story.

A historical social, every one who goes being required to wear something that symbolizes a famous event.

A portrait social, the room being hung with

pictures of distinguished people, to be named by the Endeavorers.

A joke social, each member repeating the brightest anecdote he knows, three judges deciding on the best.

A new members' social, for the purpose of obtaining new members, a select number of outsiders being especially invited.

A modelling-party, at which the Endeavorers model in clay the animals assigned them by lot, followed by a contest in guessing the names of the animals.

A proverb social, to which each Endeavorer brings two cards, on one the proverb, on the other some picture illustrating it. The whole are to be strung around the room as the basis of a guessing-contest.

A musical social, bits of music being divided into four portions, each set being distributed at haphazard. The quartettes thus formed must get together and practise, and then sing their songs before the company.

Remember that a good social does not happen. It must be planned. See that nothing is left to chance. Have a good programme ready and carry it out enthusiastically. The Intermediates' social hour, if it is properly conducted, may be made as much a part of church service as any other exercise.

CHAPTER XIII

COMMITTEES AT WORK

Flower, Pastor's Aid, Information, Sunday-School, Junior, Good Literature, Temperance and Good Citizenship, Music, Whatsoever, Delegation, Publicity

A FEW words suggesting some lines of work for other committees may be permitted.

The flower committee's work is to decorate the church and the meeting-room with flowers, which are afterward taken to the sick; and to remember the birthday of members and others with a small bouquet. This committee can make its work felt if it will mass flowers in season; have a Sunday for daisies, another when the main decoration shall be wild flowers, another for branches in blossom, and so on. The flower committee is often a calling-committee, in which case it can prepare a map of the city and a list of members' addresses.

The pastor's aid committee places its members at the disposal of the pastor to run errands or do whatever he wishes.

The information committee is expected to present at least one item of interest about Christian Endeavor work each week. *The*

Christian Endeavor World supplies abundance of material. The committee will, of course, also keep in touch with union officers and keep the society in touch with what is going on in the district. The work may also be extended so that the members may be always on the lookout for new plans and ideas for work and give the information they collect to the respective committees to use as they see fit. One new plan a month, given to each committee, would make for variety in the society.

The Sunday-school committee may invite special classes from the Sunday-school to attend the Intermediate meeting. The committee will arrange a programme in which the invited class has a part. It may try some of the following plans suggested by Professor Wells:

A canvass of the Sunday-school for new members of the Christian Endeavor society will often produce good results.

Some Christian Endeavor societies hold Sunday-school socials, to which they invite members of the Sunday-school not already in the society.

Many Sunday-school committees have found it profitable to canvass the entire town or neighborhood for young people that should be in the Sunday-school.

Where the Sunday-school carries on a home department, the Sunday-school committee will be of the greatest assistance in superintending this work or aiding the home-department superintendent.

The Sunday-school committee should become familiar with the Sunday-school library, and should from time to time call attention to its best books in the Christian Endeavor meeting.

The Sunday-school committee may occasionally distribute among the Endeavorers blank cards, asking them to fill out the cards with names of young people who they think may be persuaded to join the Sunday-school.

Whenever the Sunday-school holds special services, as at Christmas, Easter, and Children's Day, the Sunday-school committee should assist the superintendent, getting the scholars out to practice, decorating the room, and so on.

Often the teacher is not able to visit his scholars so frequently as he would like, and the Sunday-school committee should stand ready at all times to perform this service, especially in looking up the absent and calling upon the sick.

So many of our Christian Endeavor topics are in line with the Sunday-school lessons that an especial effort should be made to gather up in the Christian Endeavor meeting the best things brought out by the Sunday-school study in the morning.

Possibly the chief work of the Sunday-school committee is in supplying unexpected vacancies in the teaching force. Many a Sunday-school committee has formed itself into a normal class, studying each Sunday the lesson of the following Sunday, that the members may be ready to teach it.

The Junior committee will help the Junior superintendent and arrange for occasional joint meetings between the societies. Since Juniors graduate into the Intermediate society it is well to get acquainted beforehand. This committee may also arrange for joint socials, and should have representatives present at the Junior meeting once a month at least.

The good-literature committee will have charge of getting subscribers for Christian Endeavor and church papers, and will make a regular canvass, not only of the society, but of the church and the Sunday-school. It will gather old periodicals, and send them where they can be utilized. Discarded pictures from the Sunday-school, picture post-cards, and such like, can be used with advantage on the foreign-mission field.

Temperance and good-citizenship committees arrange for the temperance meetings, planning them carefully, and try to secure the signature of the members to a temperance pledge. The committee also gets up special talks on citizenship subjects.

The music committee has charge of the society's music, and should arrange for musical numbers at the meetings. A front-seat brigade to make the singing go with vim and vigor is a good thing to draw the members forward into those same seats. Another excellent service is to organize a musical club and a choir. One society has a number of small choirs, which take turns at singing at the evening church service. In this case it is not necessary that every member be a first-class singer. Professor Wells makes the following suggestions:

Let the society choose a society hymn expressive of its aims and ideals.

A Christian Endeavor choir may well be organized to practise the unfamiliar songs and lead the singing.

Sometimes a hymn-leader may be appointed to assist the prayer-meeting leader and have charge of the musical exercises.

Prayer-hymns may sometimes be sung most effectively with bowed heads, or even as the Endeavorers kneel at their chairs.

The work of the music committee should show in all the church services, and the Christian Endeavor choir may attend these services in a body.

Do not lay upon one Endeavorer all the work of the organist, but draft into the service all capable members, assigning them to the work month about.

Some hymns are written in the form of

question and answer, like "Watchman, tell us of the night." Assign the questions to half the room and the answers to the other half.

Once in a while begin the meeting with a song service lasting about fifteen minutes. The hymns should be arranged in a logical order and connected with comments from the leader.

The music committee may increase the interest in the song service by providing itself with anecdotes concerning the familiar hymns. These anecdotes should be given just before the hymns are sung.

Few of us have many hymns stored away in our memory, and those we know scarcely go beyond the first verse. Let the music committee set the society to committing a series of memory hymns, one for each month of the year.

To give variety in singing, occasionally have the female voices sing the stanzas and the male voices the choruses, or divide the company in other ways, asking those on the right to sing one stanza, for example, and those on the left another.

It is a good plan to select all the hymns for one evening from the work of some famous hymn-writer, an account of whose life should be given at the beginning of the meeting. Fanny Crosby, Watts, Miss Havergal, Ray Palmer, and Dr. S. F. Smith would furnish delightful evenings.

VARIOUS COMMITTEES 151

A whatsoever committee is a useful institution. One society arranged a cleaning-bee for the church, doing the cleaning both inside and out. Another carried on a reading-room ; another did janitor's work ; yet another appointed a new set of ushers each week for the church service ; and one committee planted a Christian Endeavor tree in the church back yard and tended it. This committee can have a church garden, can have charge of the church lawn, and will stand ready to do whatever the president of the society calls upon it for.

There need be no end of committees. One society has a delegation committee whose work is to visit (or rather send one of its members to visit) other societies, observe how the work is done in them, and report back to the home society. This committee also works for large delegations to attend conventions or other Christian Endeavor meetings.

A publicity committee can do a little advertising in the newspapers, and it can do a lot of good by sending its members to Junior and Young People's meetings just to advertise the Intermediate society by telling what it is doing. Members from this committee might also profitably attend the midweek prayer-meeting of the church, and tell the people there, on occasion, what the Intermediate society is trying to accomplish.

CHAPTER XIV

THINGS THAT MAY BE DONE

THE wide-awake superintendent will keep a note-book and jot down ideas for work that his society may do. The following suggestions are meant for a beginning.

THE QUIET HOUR

The Quiet Hour is designed to train Endeavorers in private devotion. The Christian ought to read his Bible and to pray every day, as the pledge points out; the Quiet Hour simply makes this pledge a little more definite by asking the young people to give a few minutes to Bible-reading and communion with God every day, preferably in the morning. The Quiet Hour covenant reads:

"Trusting in the Lord Jesus Christ for strength, I will make it the rule of my life to set apart at least fifteen minutes every day, if possible in the early morning, for quiet meditation and direct communion with God.

"Signed........................
"Date........................"

The obligation expressed in this covenant should constantly be kept before the Intermediates. A praying society must be a successful society. Covenant cards may be purchased from the United Society of Christian Endeavor, Tremont Temple, Boston, Mass.

TITHING

After the Quiet Hour comes the Tenth Legion, composed of those that promise to give a tenth of their income to the Lord. Talks on stewardship should emphasize this side of the Christian's obligations. A society whose members give tithes to the Lord is never in want of funds, and the blessing that comes to the individual members is beyond price.

The Chicago union uses the following card in its effort to secure tithers:

Please check each section which expresses your purpose thus ☒

☐ 1. My practice is to give at least ONE-TENTH of my income for Christian work.

☐ 2. I am now enrolled as a member of the TENTH LEGION.

☐ 3. I will begin now to give to Christian work at least ONE-TENTH of my income.

☐ 4. I wish to be enrolled as a member of the TENTH LEGION.

Name _____

Address _____

Society _____

Date _____

Other Pledges

There may be good reason, at times, to introduce other pledges. For instance, it may seem wise to ask the members to take a pledge to carry with them each day a copy of the New Testament, at the same time providing a small pocket-edition for this purpose. Some societies have tried a pledge for the lips, to include not only bad language, but biting and nasty words of every kind. Here is a pledge of this kind actually used by a certain society: "Trusting in the Lord Jesus Christ for strength, I promise Him that I will not repeat or tell any bad thing that I hear of any person, but will try to find all the good I can of every one, and tell it."

First-Aid Committee

A good plan is to appoint several Intermediates as the superintendent's first-aid committee, whose duty it is to do whatever they are called upon to do. Sometimes the superintendent hears of something that should be done, but cannot get into touch with the chairman of the committee under which this work would normally fall. This is a case for his first-aids. They are a sort of emergency corps.

Superintendent's At Home

An occasional social hour at the home of the superintendent works wonders. There is no necessity for elaborate preparation and a "feast," very slight refreshments being all that is called for. A talk or discussion about books or anything that interests young people, and a few games, will make all the programme that is needed.

Special Talks

The superintendent should also arrange for special talks at the regular meetings. In one society the pastor gave a brief series of talks on the history and development of the church. At another time the Intermediates listened to a college professor telling of a visit that he paid to the George Junior Republic.

Election of Officers

Some superintendents prefer to appoint the officers, and this may work in some societies. In others it might make the Intermediates feel that they were considered under age and inefficient. Usually the superintendent can advise the nominating committee. A Kansas society did something a little different when it divided into three sides, called them parties, and let them set to work. Here is the plan:

Three groups of six members each were selected to constitute political parties, the Reds, Whites, and Blues.

Each side met and made out a slate of names for officers, and campaigned for its slate.

The election was held in booths erected for the purpose, judges and clerks having been appointed to take care of the details. It goes without saying that the members of the society were interested in the outcome. There is something in politics that liberates enthusiasm.

Of course this method must not be used where there is a chance of unkind feelings' being aroused.

Intermediate Brotherhood

A superintendent of a boys' Intermediate society writes that he finds the plan to organize the boys under a male leader, and the girls under a woman, works well in his church. The boys' society is called the Intermediate Brotherhood of Christian Endeavor.

Wall Mottoes

The society should have a standing motto, of course, but besides this the members will be glad to make mottoes for the walls. These mottoes can be frequently changed.

Clubs

Walking clubs, tennis clubs, and clubs for sports of various kinds are a help, especially during the summer months. The little book issued by the United Society of Christian Endeavor, Tremont Temple, Boston, Mass., "Successful Boys' Clubs," contains abundant material for this side of work with boys.

A President's Bible

The society may contribute toward a Bible which shall be given to the president and used by him as long as he is in office. When he ceases to be president, he will give the Bible to his successor. The names of the presidents, and the time they held office, should be printed on the fly-leaf of the Bible.

Flying Squadron

Organize a committee called the flying squadron, with four or five members, whose duty (and delight) it will be to visit, one Sunday a month, some other Intermediate society and take part in the meeting. If there are no Intermediate societies near, let the squadron visit a Young People's society and boost Intermediate work.

A Ten-Cent Investment

Give each member, out of the funds of the society, if necessary, ten cents with which to trade for a month or two, the profits and the original capital, of course, to go into the society's funds. Have a social hour at the end of the period, when each member will tell how he earned the money he brings.

Roll-Call

A society banished stiffness at the monthly roll-call by abolishing it entirely for a month or two. Cards were distributed among the members, reminding them that the following Sunday was consecration-meeting, and recalling the requirements of the pledge. The members were asked to sign the cards and drop them into a box at the meeting. This gave the secretary a record of the attendance. There was no roll-call, but every one took part in the meeting.

Lafalot Club

A young man in the Hartford, Conn., union, started a " Lafalot Club," which really is a kind of social committee. The members pledge themselves to laugh a lot, and they have hikes together, games, and real good times.

"Be Brave" Brigade

The members of this brigade pledge themselves to try to do right at all times. They have patriotic exercises, salutation of the flag, singing of patriotic songs, and so forth.

Consecration-Meetings

Here are some simple ways to vary the consecration-meetings:

THINGS THAT MAY BE DONE 159

At a prayer consecration-meeting there is no speaking, but each Endeavorer offers prayer.

Special pains should be taken to obtain from absentees not merely brief messages, but helpful and attractive letters.

At a "next-step" consecration-meeting each member agrees to take part in some way more difficult for him than usual.

At a committee consecration-meeting the roll of the committees is called. Each committee stands and testifies, the chairman leading.

At a "C. E." consecration-meeting each Endeavorer brings two texts beginning with those initials and embodying his prayer for the coming month.

Have the secretary, instead of calling the roll in the usual way, call the letters of the alphabet. After each letter all whose names begin with that letter will take part.

It is well occasionally to hold what may be called a "definite" consecration-meeting, each Endeavorer consecrating himself to one definite task for the coming month.

The consecration-meeting held after election of officers and committees should have especial reference to that event, and be a consecration to special lines of society work.

Sometimes have the society testify in the consecration-meeting without a roll-call, the leader calling upon the different sections of the room in turn, and asking the members to speak in the order in which they sit.

A voluntary consecration-meeting is conducted without a roll-call, the secretary noting who takes part. At the close of the meeting the roll may be called if necessary, those answering, "Present" that have already taken part.

It is possible to dispense with the calling of the roll if each member has a printed list of the entire membership. If a member is absent, the secretary calls his name, and the one next in order immediately takes part.

The best arrangement of a society for missionary work is a division into bands, one for the study of each missionary topic of the year. Where this division exists, it may be made the basis of a consecration-meeting, each band testifying in turn.

Reserved Seats in Church

The pastor will probably be glad occasionally to speak to young people, and at these times a number of seats should be reserved for the Intermediates, who will take pride in filling them. Again, a number of seats for the Sunday-evening church service might be reserved for the Intermediates to fill by coming themselves and bringing their friends. If this is well

THINGS THAT MAY BE DONE 161

worked and boomed, it should increase the attendance.

FIRESIDE SOCIAL

On Sunday afternoons a Boston church holds an informal fireside social. The young people gather around a big fire in a cozy room, and have music, story-telling, discussion of books recently read, and so forth. No programme is prepared for this meeting, but each one does what he can. After the social the young people adjourn to another room for light refreshments, and then go to the Christian Endeavor meeting. This social time has been a great boon to roomers, and is thoroughly enjoyed.

CHAIN PRAYER

No better method than chain prayer can be found to help young people to take part in the meetings. Always have these prayers after the topic has been discussed, so that the members will have something, suggested by the topic, to pray about. Put a timid Intermediate between two older members, and get the one to pray before him and the other after him. Rigidly confine these chain prayers to one sentence.

DISORDER IN MEETING

Try the plan of having the parents of some of the Intermediates present at every meeting. Do not have too many at once, however.

Commission Government

When the officers fail to do their duty, try the plan of commission government. Divide the work of all officials into four branches; assign one commissioner to each branch, and make one of the four president. Each commissioner will appoint assistants who will form the working committees of the society.

Prayer Clubs

A society in California has two clubs or prayer circles, one for the boys and one for the girls. They meet separately, and this fact removes any restraint that any one might feel about taking part. The meetings are informal. About twenty minutes are spent in Bible drill and singing; then about ten minutes in prayer, the lights being turned down so that each one may feel free to take part. Sometimes the boys tell their experiences in trying to reach and help other boys. At the close they all stand with arms locked and pray in turn. This plan is making a strong society out of one that looked like a failure before the clubs were started.

Serenading Party

A superintendent who believed that the Intermediates ought to attend the midweek services of the church arranged, after the last prayer-meeting of the month, to have the Inter-

THINGS THAT MAY BE DONE 163

mediates go and serenade six or seven shut-ins. Only members that had attended three prayer-meetings during the month were allowed in the serenading party. Each week a short practice was held at the close of the midweek prayer-meeting.

Fruit for the Sick

Societies may carry fruit for the sick and find pleasure in preparing for this service. They should make pasteboard boxes covered with colored tissue-paper, and decorated tastefully, in which to carry the fruit.

Alphabetical Socials

To secure the wherewithal to help the poor at Christmas time a society arranged alphabetical socials, each member being asked to bring groceries and clothing beginning with the first letter of his surname.

Bible Questions

Prepare a list of Bible questions, fifty or sixty of them, and thoroughly drill the Intermediates in them. If the pastor be willing, the drill may then be given at an evening church service. Let the superintendent stand at the back of the hall and put the questions, so that every one present may hear. It will be a wonder if the Intermediates' knowledge does not far exceed that of church-members present.

164 THE INTERMEDIATE MANUAL

Special Meetings

One society tried an Easter meeting at 6:30 A. M., instead of in the evening, and it proved a great success. This society arranged the chairs differently at some meetings for the sake of variety. Thus they were arranged to form the word "W I N" at a missionary meeting. At other times they have been made to form the Christian Endeavor monogram, or have been placed in a circle.

Intermediate Graduation

The graduates were seated on the platform, the Juniors in the choir-loft just behind the platform.

Stretching across the platform, immediately behind the graduates, was a large arch made of muslin a foot broad and divided into seven sections by means of small strips of drab-colored paper representing cement. The fourth section formed the centre of the arch.

In the spaces were the following words, cut out of thin black paper and pasted on the muslin: (1) Strive; (2) Pray; (3) Read the Bible; (4) Promise Him; (5) Lead a Christian Life; (6) Be Present; (7) Take Part.

Both societies, Junior and Intermediate, took part in the opening exercises. Then the graduates repeated the Intermediate pledge.

All sat down except number four, who had

THINGS THAT MAY BE DONE 165

the part, "I promise Him." She said: "As the centre and strength of the arch is the keystone, so the centre and strength of our pledge is the covenant, 'I promise Him.'" She then sang a song about the promise, and closed by saying: "Take away the keystone, and the arch will fall; take away the pledge, and the society will cease to exist. By prayer and reading the Bible we are taught to strive."

Number one gave a verse about striving; number two, a recitation on prayer; number three, the song, "Holy Bible, book divine"; number five had something to say on Christian living; and numbers six and seven gave short talks on being present and taking part. Each graduate remained standing after taking part.

Then followed the distribution of diplomas and an address of welcome by the president of the Young People's society.

The idea was worked out by Miss Pearl Page, Junior superintendent of the Lutheran society, Shiloh, O.

Special Topic Cards

Get up special topic cards with topics, the pledge, the names of members, and the committees on which they serve.

Object-Talks

Plan to have an object-talk at each meeting. The Intermediates will give the talks if the subject is selected for them. This feature is worth the attention of the superintendent and the prayer-meeting committee. The illustrations used at the meetings should be chosen from school life or from circles that interest the boys and girls.

Some Suggested Committees

If there is need for them the following committees may help to make the work effectual. No society, of course, will have all the committees here named. Besides the ordinary committees we might have a committee on civics, a visitation committee, literary, strangers', entertainment, programme, notices, religious-work, church-attendance, ushers', athletic, vestibule, order, ways-and-means, social-service, printing, sermon, advertising, and press committees.

Things to Study

Very often the Intermediates may want to attack some of the great problems that trouble our day. If they do, themes like the following form food for study:

Child labor, women in industry, wealth and poverty, labor movements, civic corruption and its cure, housing of the poor, public utilities, immigration, foreign relations, race problems, prison reform, intemperance, divorce, the peace movement, pure food, the cigarette, first aid to

THINGS THAT MAY BE DONE 167

the wounded, and all nature studies. It is not well, however, to press these subjects upon Intermediates. They will have to face them soon enough.

THINGS TO DO

One might have Intermediate Bible classes in the Sunday-school; get the society to visit hospitals and homes, and sing for the inmates; help in mission services; invite people to come to church by card and otherwise; form a choir and sing at church; conduct boys' clubs; have athletic sports; get up lectures; watch the action of the city council and thus arouse civic interest; study playgrounds and streets; have debates; study parliamentary practice; get up a glee club; report cases of sickness; have membership contests; organize a telephone corps to increase attendance at meetings; have a messenger service for the pastor's benefit; prepare for special days, Mothers' Day, Memorial Day, Thanksgiving, Christmas, Old Folks' Day; collect a missionary library; have the Intermediates work with Juniors and be Big Brothers; have a newcomers' bureau to see that newcomers are visited and invited to the meeting and to church; leave invitations to church in hotels and boarding-houses.

The first condition for success in an Intermediate society is to have plenty of work for every member. The boys and girls of Intermediate age are full of enthusiasm. They want to do things worth while. If they are left idle, they will gravitate toward the outside of the society; but, if things are doing all the time, they will want to be in the thick of the bustle. The superintendent that understands this, and is willing to plan for each member, may go in and win.

CHAPTER XV

INCREASING EFFICIENCY

THE Intermediates belong to a new generation of Endeavorers. Many of them come, of course, from the Junior society and are well versed in the methods of that group; but all Intermediates need to be schooled in the fundamental principles of Christian Endeavor and instructed as to its methods of work. Only careful training along these lines can make effective workers and efficient societies.

As in day school we have text-books, so also in Christian Endeavor. It would be folly to try to teach day-school pupils without the help of books. Yet this is what is often attempted in Christian Endeavor societies. It cannot be done. We must make use of every printed help that we can find and that we can induce Intermediates to study. And there are printed helps a plenty. The United Society exists for the purpose of providing such helps. Every officer, every committee, may find greatly needed suggestions in book and pamphlet and chart. The Intermediate society follows as a rule the plans of the Young People's society. It is forward-looking. It is preparing for just the kind of tasks that the Young People's society is doing. It should therefore use the helps designed for the Young People's society.

One of the best helps for keying up the society and for suggesting lines of work is the Christian Endeavor Efficiency Chart. This chart outlines the work that should be done by an efficient society. It is valuable because it reveals to the society wherein it is falling short. Sometimes we complacently imagine that we are doing finely when in fact we are not doing half the work we ought to be doing. When a society compares its actual work with the work suggested by the chart, its real condition is brought home to it, and it is spurred to do better.

Increase and Efficiency Standards

The first thing to do is to secure an Increase and Efficiency Chart from the United Society of Christian Endeavor, Boston, Mass.

This beautiful wall chart divides the work of the society into three sections: first, society organization; second, individual training; third, missionary service at home and abroad. Each section is subdivided into ten divisions, and ten points are given for the work in each subdivision, making 100 points for each section. In the centre of the chart is a thermometer on which the progress of the society toward the goal, 300 per cent, may be traced.

In the first section of the chart the work of the various committees and the general organization

INCREASING EFFICIENCY 171

of the society are outlined; in the second section the things that individual Endeavorers may do, including the Quiet Hour, Tenth Legion, testimony, prayer, leaders, and so on; in the third section we have missionary work and social service. The chart is a magnificent programme. It is full of suggestions. And it is a test of efficiency.

How to Test the Society

It is a very simple matter to take the rating of the society with the aid of the Efficiency Chart. The executive committee goes over the chart item by item and asks whether the work indicated is being done by the society. If it is being done, then small seals are attached to the chart opposite the work done. When the committee has gone over the entire chart in this way, count up the number of points indicated by the seals, and that number will represent the society's rating. Some societies will find that they can claim only fifty points out of a possible three hundred. Others will do better than this. Some may do worse. But no society should be discouraged because its rating is low. The thing to do is to start on a campaign to increase it. How may this be done?

Let the executive committee pick out the things that the society may easily do and start on them. Go from the easy to the more difficult tasks. Gradually the thermometer will climb and the

Intermediates will be interested in making it climb quickly. They will have something definite to work for. They will have definite work to do. The rating should be taken every month and progress indicated on the chart.

It is a good plan to appoint an Efficiency superintendent who will have charge of the chart and whose work it will be to boost it and encourage the members to heroic endeavors.

Beware of trying to do everything that the chart suggests at once. One step at a time brings us to the goal. Begin with the fundamental things. See that your executive committee is on its job, doing what it is intended to do. Test this committee's work by that section of the chart that deals with it. Select parts from the section on individual training. As a house is built by placing stone on stone, so is a society built up gradually.

No society is too small to use the chart, for no society is too small to be made better.

Some societies have found that they do best when they concentrate for a time on one section of the chart. Thus, for instance, for one month or two months they will concentrate on the section that deals with individual training and encourage the Intermediates to become church members, to practise the Quiet Hour, to take part in public prayer, to offer original testimony in the meetings, to lead meetings, to become soul-winners, to give a definite part of their income to the Lord's work, to attend church services, to become Life-Work Recruits (that is, dedicate their lives to full-time Christian service as ministers, missionaries, and so on), and to become Christian Endeavor Experts. By concentrating on these points the society's rating will mount rapidly, but better than that, the Intermediates will be getting training in useful work.

Another month or two is given to intensive work on one of the other sections, say, the section on society organization, and the attention of the whole society is then directed toward building up the committees and carrying out their various programmes.

The Efficiency Chart should always be hung in a prominent place in the prayer-meeting room, and the Intermediates should never be permitted to forget it.

If desired, the society may be divided into two sides and a contest may be started on the individual-training section, or on certain parts of it.

A debate may be tried on a subject like this: Resolved, that the individual-training section of the Efficiency chart is more important than the missionary section. Three speakers on each side should be selected to present the arguments.

Expert Endeavorers

Many societies are recruited from groups of young people who have not been trained in a Junior society, and it is common to hear Intermediates ask, What are the duties of the president, or the vice-president, or the secretary? What is the work of the prayer-meeting committee, the lookout committee, and so forth?

The most concise answer to these questions is given in a series of Efficiency leaflets by Professor Amos R. Wells. There is a leaflet for each officer in the society, one on the work of each committee, and leaflets on the history of Christian Endeavor, the pledge, and the prayer meeting. Each member of the society should be given the three latter leaflets to study at home, a quiz being held in the society on the contents. One leaflet may be given out each week for three weeks. Then to every officer in the society and to every member of each committee should be given the leaflets dealing with their work or the work of the committee to which they belong. In this way a general idea of the working of the society may be imparted to all the members, and many will be encouraged to ask for more information.

These leaflets are bound into one volume called "Expert Endeavor." The degree of "Christian Endeavor Expert" is granted by the United Society of Christian Endeavor to Endeavorers that study the book and pass an examination on it.

A good plan is to adopt "Expert Endeavor" as a text-book and start a class. The leader of the class need not be an expert teacher; all that is necessary is that he be able to inspire the members of the class to do real work and master the

INCREASING EFFICIENCY 175

contents of the book. An Intermediate superintendent will find no better method of training his young people than by organizing and teaching such a class.

The class may meet weekly or every two weeks. It may consist of few or many. The officers and chairmen of committees should in any case take the course, but it will greatly add to the efficiency of the society if all the members take it.

The examining committee is appointed by the society, and it is suggested that the pastor and Intermediate superintendent serve as members of this committee. Examinations may be oral or written — written examinations are most thorough. Each member of the class should be asked at least one hundred questions covering the entire book. To pass he must attain a rating, which is fixed by the examining committee, of at least 75 per cent. The names of those that pass, with their ratings, should be sent to the United Society of Christian Endeavor, Boston, Mass., and Expert certificates will be sent them.

For those that wish fuller information about the work of Christian Endeavor helps of all kinds are published.

Recreation and Efficiency

The place and value of play in the lives of Intermediates have not been sufficiently recognized. The teen age is the age of abounding energy which seeks physical expression. The community and the church have both scored a melancholy failure by neglecting to organize the play of our boys and girls. The street, the back alley, and the vacant lot are often the only places where young people can play, unless they choose the various forms of commercialized amusement, the dance hall, the moving-picture show, and the pool-room.

Recreation stirs Intermediates along the line of their interests and may easily be made a means of winning new members to the society. Recreation is what Intermediates *want* as well as what they need; religion, the activities of Christian Endeavor, are what the Intermediates *need*, but do not always want. We must show them that religion means an all-round development, physical, mental, and spiritual. The Intermediate society should be as much interested in the Intermediates' play as in their souls; indeed, play and the soul's welfare are one thing and not two things.

Let the superintendent appoint a recreation committee in the society and with the committee work out a programme which may be applied in the local conditions. Secure the helps on Christian Endeavor recreation which the United Society of Christian Endeavor, Boston, Mass., has published, and from the suggestions contained in these helps draw up the programme.

Perhaps the social committee may be expanded into a social and recreation committee.

A good beginning for a recreational programme

would be for the social and recreation committee to secure, if possible, a room in the church for recreational purposes. Many churches will gladly open their doors for this kind of thing, and to do so makes the church recognize its responsibility for the play activities of its young people. These are the facts that the superintendent or the friend of the young people may present:

1. The church is responsible for the play of its young people.

2. The church should supervise and guide the play of its young people.

Few churches will care to deny the church's responsibility in these matters, and if responsibility is admitted, then the question becomes a practical one: what can we do to supervise, guide, and provide a place for recreation for our young folks?

Intermediate recreation should be supervised. The superintendent will say that he is already overburdened and cannot accept this additional responsibility. Well! This is a church problem. What is to hinder the members of the men's Bible class, who are always looking for work to do, from taking turns in supervising the recreational hours? And why should not the members of the ladies' Bible class give their services as hostesses on the evenings when the Christian Endeavor room is open? This would interest the older people of the church in Intermediate work and provide worth-while tasks for some of our church members.

The Christian Endeavor room should be furnished by the society. It may have games such as checkers, crokinole, chess, and dominoes. A corner may be fitted up for writing. In some cases the room may contain a gramophone and a piano. It should be open one or two nights a week, or, if supervision is plentiful, it may be open every night.

The Intermediates may be given the use of the church basement for athletics and games. They should buy their own equipment, dumb bells, Indian clubs, wall-pulley weights, wall springs, apparatus for weight-lifting, indoor baseball, basket ball, and so forth. There should be one or two ropes for climbing, perhaps a horizontal bar, some swinging rings, and so forth. The loose apparatus should always be placed in lockers when not in use.

The society should have a custodian who will look after the safe keeping of the apparatus.

Indoor games may be played on certain nights, under proper supervision. One might suggest volley ball, indoor baseball, roller skating.

But recreation may be carried out even better out-of-doors, winter and summer. Besides the games mentioned there are football, baseball, hockey, tennis, golf, and others.

Teams may be formed in the society and inter-team games may be played. Other societies may be challenged to a tournament.

Then there are skating, coasting, ice-boating,